RETIREMENT PLANNING
for Young Physicians

Dr. Ralph P. Crew

The information, ideas, and suggestions in this book are not intended to render professional advice. Before following any suggestions contained in this book, you should consult your personal accountant or other financial advisor. Neither the author nor the publisher shall be liable or responsible for any loss or damage allegedly arising as a consequence of your use or application of any information or suggestions in this book.

The information, ideas, and suggestions in this book are not intended as a substitute for professional medical advice. Before following any suggestions contained in this book, you should consult your personal physician. Neither the author nor the publisher shall be liable or responsible for any loss or damage allegedly arising as a consequence of your use or application of any information or suggestions in this book.

LifeRich Publishing is a registered trademark of The Reader's Digest Association, Inc.

LifeRich Publishing books may be ordered through booksellers or by contacting:

LifeRich Publishing
1663 Liberty Drive
Bloomington, IN 47403
www.liferichpublishing.com
1 (888) 238-8637

Because of the dynamic nature of the Internet, any web addresses or links contained in this book may have changed since publication and may no longer be valid. The views expressed in this work are solely those of the author and do not necessarily reflect the views of the publisher, and the publisher hereby disclaims any responsibility for them.

Any people depicted in stock imagery provided by Thinkstock are models, and such images are being used for illustrative purposes only.
Certain stock imagery © Thinkstock.

ISBN: 978-1-4897-1457-2 (sc)
ISBN: 978-1-4897-1456-5 (hc)
ISBN: 978-1-4897-1458-9 (e)

Library of Congress Control Number: 2017918556

Print information available on the last page.

LifeRich Publishing rev. date: 12/6/2017

For Kay and her lifelong support.

Contents

Introduction

For years I have discussed with medical students and residents their financial futures. I review the benefits of planning their careers and emphasize the need to be committed to a formal financial strategy. I am not a trained financial advisor. What I impart in this book is knowledge obtained through life experience and research. I am trying to teach important investing and life skills that will serve young physicians for the rest of their lives. Before making any investments, do your homework. Don't just trust me.

The physicians of my generation have been blessed. We have practiced through a period of prosperity, good reimbursement, reasonable regulation, and affordable overhead. As self-employed individuals, we have been able to take advantage of the many tax breaks available to business. These features have allowed many physicians to accumulate significant wealth, a large portion of which is maintained in tax-deferred retirement plans.

The health-care industry is changing. Many of these wealth-creating benefits will not be available to future medical school graduates. Physician reimbursement has been flat for the past decade. It is unlikely that physicians will be paid more in the future. Most graduating physicians are now employed by larger medical groups or hospital systems. Increased regulation, bureaucracy, and electronic medical records reduce productivity and increase overhead. In the past, physicians were able to accumulate wealth without great effort. Physicians in the future will need to execute financial and lifestyle planning to become financially independent.

Many of my peers have been able to acquire very prosperous lifestyles. Large homes, premium automobiles, expensive vacations, private schools for children, and second homes are common. This lifestyle is enticing. It can become a priority in one's life. But if improperly managed, it can become a house of cards affecting relationships, health, and retirement. It will be limited to only a few physicians in the future.

For most specialties, the opportunity to create significant affluence is fading. Flat wages and inflation have resulted in real income being stagnant. Changes in reimbursement, regulation, productivity, and employment are only going to continue this trend. Financial planning is becoming more essential for new physicians to attain their dreams of financial independence.

Perhaps the greatest reason for a financial strategy is retirement. You will probably live another twenty-five to thirty years after you retire. How will this be funded? Due to the length of your education, by the time you start practicing, you will be almost a decade behind in retirement contributions. It takes time for significant assets to accrue. The earlier you get started, the better. Larger, more consistent contributions will be required to catch up and produce retirement incomes commensurate with your working lifestyle.

No one knows when he or she will retire. It is impossible to completely fund a successful retirement with a 401(k)/403(b), the standard retirement programs for hospital and employed physicians. Additional savings will have to occur, through other retirement plans, after-tax savings, and lifestyle adjustments. It is quite possible that you will need to work as much as a decade longer than my generation. Optimization of physical and mental health will be required. Prudent lifestyles will be essential.

In the following chapters I will discuss these concepts in greater depth and assist you in creating a financial and lifestyle plan leading to a lifetime of prosperity.

1

When Will I Retire?

It was estimated in 2012 that 26 percent of practicing physicians were sixty years old or older.[1] A quarter of all physicians are approaching retirement! When should a physician retire? Why should you retire? Did you know that physicians tend to work longer than their peers? Although some of us will continue to work until we die, most of us aspire to a period of retirement at the end of our busy careers, a time in which to enjoy the hobbies we've neglected or perhaps start new ones. We want time to enjoy our grandchildren, travel, learn a new language, or just sit around at home reading. Today there isn't enough time to fiddle in the workshop or perfect Grandma's recipes. We will do that when we retire.

Those of us in our sixties and seventies have had wonderful careers. We have lived through amazing changes in health care. Payments for our services were generous, overhead manageable, and cost of living reasonable. Institutional and community respect for physicians was high. Financial instruments were developed for us to accumulate wealth. New retirement plans maximized tax advantages. Most of us owned our own practices. Many owned the buildings within which their practices were housed. But times have changed.

Those of you in medical school or residency now will have a markedly different practice environment, in some ways better but in many ways more complicated and challenging. These challenges will affect all aspects of practice but will become most notable when you reach retirement age. When would you like to retire? That's an unfair question to ask an individual in his or her thirties. There are too many variables, the most important of which is this: when will I be able to afford to retire?

When I turned sixty, I fully expected to practice into my seventies. My health was good, and I enjoyed what I was doing. At age sixty-three, my outlook changed, and I decided to sell my practice. Our local hospital had been sold to a large corporation. I was frustrated by electronic medical records and increasing paperwork. Medicare was instituting bureaucratic payment reforms. I was working like a madman, often seeing over fifty patients a day. My wife and I wanted to see more of our grandchildren, and I had some hobbies that needed attention. One day, I had an epiphany and realized that with the sale of my practice and the sufficient funds in my retirement plan, I could support my wife and me for the rest of our lives. The questions then became: Why am I working? What do I want to do with the rest of my life? A period of soul-searching ensued, ending with the decision to continue practicing medicine but with a new, part-time emphasis: teaching residents surgery and clinical medicine. One or two days a week, I work with residents, and the remaining time is mine.

My retirement decision was cemented when my partner purchased my half of the practice. As a result, I would receive income monthly for the next seven years and would not have to access my retirement savings. Why continue to work?

It is impossible to predict when you will be ready for retirement. Many factors must be taken into consideration. By far, the most important deciding issue will be whether you have enough money. Once you have sufficient savings, everything else will fall in place. It's freedom. If you enjoy medicine but are tired of the grind, you can decrease your hours or change your job. Perhaps it's time to serve on a mission trip overseas or work in an indigent clinic. There are plenty of opportunities for physicians to work a relaxed schedule and continue to share their skills and enthusiasm. It could be time to get out of medicine entirely, develop new skills or hobbies, or perhaps travel around the world. Once you have the money, you'll get to make the decisions. No one else will control your life. You can sleep in or stay up all night reading.

Many of you will retire early. This could be by your own choice or necessitated by health or family issues. Most of the time, it's not something you can foresee. A Transamerica Center for Retirement Study reports that 60 percent of retirees left the workforce earlier than planned.[2] Thirty-seven percent left due to health issues. Only 16 percent retired early because they could afford it. Fifty-one percent of workers expect to work in retirement.[3]

Tremendous changes are occurring in all aspects of medicine, creating new kinds of stress for physicians. Many are reconsidering their careers. According to the 2016 Merritt Hawkins Survey of America's Physicians, half of physicians over forty-five and 41 percent of younger physicians have expedited their retirement plans due to these changes.[4] These feelings are higher in self-employed physicians and specialists. Retirement is clearly on the minds of many physicians.

The assumptions in this book are dependent on thirty-five years of retirement savings. If these contributions are truncated, there will be less money with which to retire. Some critics may say that my savings suggestions are too aggressive and will result in surplus retirement savings. The White Coat Advisor claims, after extensive calculations, that you will need only 28 percent of your income in retirement.[5] He neglects the fact that the future growth of wages will be flat and ignores the deleterious effects of inflation. Considering the large number of individuals who will need to retire early, it is best to err on the excessive side of saving. Gallup reported in April 2014 that 59 percent of

Americans were concerned about having enough money for retirement.[6] No one wants to run out of money! If you end up having too much money, I am certain you will be able to find something to do with it. Perhaps you will retire a few years early, as I did.

According to a 2016 study of AMA Insurance, the number one financial concern of physicians of all ages is having enough money to retire. Thirty-nine percent of physicians report that they are behind in saving for retirement.[7] That same report indicates that there are seven characteristics common to physicians who are adequately preparing for retirement:

1. Knowledge of personal finance
2. Use of a professional financial advisor
3. Less consumer debt
4. "Maxing out" 401(k)/403(b) contributions annually
5. Having estate plans in place
6. Confidence in their decision-making
7. Having a plan to retire sooner

Physicians have difficulty achieving these goals. Just 45 percent in their thirties have a financial advisor. Only 37 percent of physicians in their sixties are without debt, and 35 percent of all physicians have no elements of an estate plan. A third of physicians in their thirties plan to retire before the age of sixty-five, but less than two-thirds max out their 401(k)/403(b) yearly. Sadly, only two-thirds of doctors in their fifties maximize 401(k)/403(b) contributions! How can you expect to retire comfortably if you are not prepared?

Hopefully, this book will put you on track to fulfill these characteristics yourself, allowing you to be confident in your financial decisions for retirement.

A major concern is that many of the current generation of physicians completing training (i.e., you) will have limited ability to acquire the financial resources needed to retire at a reasonable age and lifestyle. Many of the advantages my generation experienced will not be available to or will be reduced for recent graduates. As Yogi Berra once said, "The future ain't what it used to be."[8] I will attempt to quantify the significance of these deficits and offer some solutions. Everyone's situation is unique. Some of you will earn large salaries that preclude some of my concerns, and others among you may have a spouse who will augment your finances. In all cases you will still need to plan and save significant sums of money for retirement, more than you ever expected. I will be using a salary of $220,000 in my examples. You can easily extrapolate if your income is different. By the way, with this salary, you are one of the top 0.04 percent richest people in the world. It would take the average laborer in Indonesia 296 years to earn the same amount.[9] You are blessed!

2

The Minimum You Will Need to Retire

My decision to retire came quickly. It's likely you will have a similar experience. It's difficult to predict the future—no, impossible! It's important to be prepared. Actuarially, most physicians will live into their eighties, perhaps even into their nineties.[1] According to the Social Security Administration, the average male reaching sixty-five today will live until 84.3, and the average woman will live until 86.6 years of age.[2] One out of every four sixty-five-year-olds alive today will live past ninety! One in ten will live past ninety-five. As a physician living a healthy lifestyle, you could well be one of these. If your retirement savings are used up before you die, you will likely live in poverty. Social Security's maximum payment in 2017 is only $2,687 per month ($32,244 a year).[3] Difficult to survive on that! My health insurance in retirement costs $22,016 a year. The income you will live on depends on how much you have saved. Fortunately, I saved enough. Will you?

For years retirement planners have counseled individuals that they will need 70 to 80 percent of their preretirement income in retirement. Obviously, this number is quite variable and depends on lifestyle and health. Recently, the Employee Benefit Research Institute determined that 46 percent of households actually spent more money in their first two years of retirement. This trend lasted for six years in a third of retirees and was consistent across all income levels.[3]

None of us knows how long we will live or what our health will be. We cannot predict whether we will need to retire early or whether we will be able to work years beyond the normal retirement age. But in all cases, sufficient funds need to be available for a comfortable future. These assets can come from many sources, including the sale of a practice, formal retirement plans, and independent investing. There may need to be a change in lifestyle to allow the existing funds to last. Later, I will make calculations and evaluate the methods and savings required to attain a comfortable retirement.

The income you will require in retirement is dependent on two components: fixed and variable expenses. Fixed expenses are those that cannot be avoided. They remain the same regardless of changes in employment or lifestyle. Examples are utilities, insurance, mortgage, and taxes. Variable expenses change with your fluctuations in lifestyle, such as vacations, eating out at restaurants, and money spent on hobbies. You have to pay the fixed expenses, or else they will turn off your water or foreclose on your house. Variable expenses can be adjusted according to the assets available to be spent on them. Both can be adjusted and are dependent on you. For instance, the fixed costs for a $600,000 home will be different than those for a $300,000 home. The taxes, insurance, mortgage, maintenance, and utilities all will be higher for a larger home. As you approach retirement, it is beneficial to reduce your fixed costs, making it easier to live on a limited income. Perhaps you replace your home with a more modest version or move to a state with lower property taxes. Get rid of your landline. Own only one car or wait to retire until you are Medicare-eligible so that you can have lower health insurance premiums. At least try to pay off your existing mortgage prior to retirement, since that is probably your largest fixed cost. Once your fixed costs are managed, you will be able to determine how much you can spend on the fun parts of retirement such as trips, hobbies, grandchildren, and dining out.

To get a realistic view of expenses in retirement, here are my fixed expenses for the last year.

Mortgage (none)	0
Automobile payments (none)	0
Property taxes on home	$5,640
License plate fees	$159
Insurance	
Home	$950
Automobile (two vehicles)	$1,600
Umbrella	$697
Health (not on Medicare yet)	$22,016
Utilities	
Gas	$1,092
Electric	$1,226
Water and sewage	$536
Cell phones	$750
Cable, internet, landline	$2,304
Security system	$640
Total fixed costs	$37,610

Almost $40,000 a year for the basic necessities! This is without mortgage obligations or automobile payments. Food also is not included, nor is the gasoline to run our cars. Most of these fixed expenses are difficult to reduce without major changes in lifestyle. Could you function in today's world without a cell phone or internet? Would you dare go without health insurance? Keep in mind that even though I do not have a mortgage, home maintenance can be a considerable expense. Last month I spent $10,000 to replace my driveway and back patio. One of my vehicles is eleven years old and will soon need to be replaced. Maintenance expenses can be significant with older vehicles, particularly if they are premium models such as BMWs or Mercedes. I live in a modest home in a state with high property taxes. Our largest fixed expense is health insurance, and the expense I have listed doesn't include the copays and deductibles I paid this past year. Fortunately, this cost will decline next year when my wife and I become eligible for Medicare.

Our largest variable expenses by far are charitable donations and gifts to our family. Expenses for food, entertainment, charity, and trips can vary from small amounts to tens of thousands a year. This is where you will find the greatest ability to control your cost of living in retirement. Look closely to determine which indulgences you can afford and which you cannot.

Let's extrapolate my fixed expenses to the year 2052, thirty-five years from now, when you will be ready to retire. Your expenses will likely be similar to mine. The average rate of inflation over the past century has been about 3.2 percent.[4] If I apply that growth rate to my fixed expenses, they become approximately $113,000 in 2052.[5] Makes you think, doesn't it? You will need a boatload of money when you retire just to pay for these costs. Current formulas suggest that your retirement savings should be twenty-five times the amount you will be spending yearly in retirement ($113,000 x 25 = $2,825,000). So in 2052 you will need almost three million dollars in your account just to pay for your modest fixed expenses. Variable spending will require significant additional resources. We'll talk about this in greater depth later.

Thankfully, many of the expenses we have during our careers should be reduced or absent by the time we retire, including the following:

- Income taxes (lower income means less taxes)
- Child care
- Health insurance (Medicare is less expensive than commercial health insurance)
- Medical school loans
- Expenses related to work (clothing, lunches, and commuting)
- Mortgage

- Disability or life insurance
- Retirement plan contributions
- Charitable giving (the amount you give may decrease if you calculate donations as a percentage of your income)

3

Owning Your Own Practice

Acquiring the large sums required for a comfortable retirement will be difficult. Compared with the retirement of my peers, it is possible that your retirement will be delayed by almost a decade to achieve financial security. How can that be? It doesn't sound fair! Many factors prevalent in society and health care today are responsible.

Physicians of my generation and earlier were primarily self-employed. Current graduates, with a few exceptions, will work for large groups or hospital systems. Being self-employed has its advantages and disadvantages, but the benefits of being a small business person are extensive. Consider how being your own boss, setting your hours, and selecting your employees could make your life easier. Being able to institute new programs or buy equipment without months of meetings and groveling to the administration is empowering. The financial benefits of running expenses through a practice are the backbone of American business.

It is quite possible that you will live as long in retirement as you practiced medicine. That's a long time! You will need a lot of money! The only way to be financially prepared is to acquire significant assets during the working phase of your life. Your ability to do this as a hospital employee will be limited. Small business—that is, private practice—allows for many opportunities to accumulate wealth. The US tax code was specifically written for business. These regulations allow businesses to thrive and grow. When you work for someone else, they have those advantages, not you.

Presently, only 22 percent of physicians in their thirties are self-employed or partners in a medical group. This compares to over 50 percent of doctors over sixty.[1] The following items enhance retirement planning and build wealth for self-employed physicians, and they are not generally available to employed physicians:

- Sale of a practice
- Sale of practice equipment
- Sale or lease of practice-related real estate
- Sale or lease of surgical center
- Sale of practice-related businesses (optical, hearing aids, lab, etc.)
- Defined contribution retirement plan income deferral up to $54,000 (2017)
- Defined benefit retirement plan

Selling a practice is a wonderful way to augment retirement savings and income. The value of a practice varies depending on profitability, size, location, and specialty. Some are worth only thousands of dollars, others millions. Your generation of physicians will have little opportunity to benefit. The number of independent practices is rapidly declining as a result of hospital systems purchasing them and the lack of interest in private practice by new doctors. How many opportunities will there be to sell your practice thirty-five years from now? Impossible to determine. There is certainly a need to improve quality and productivity in health care. Privately owned practices offer some advantages in these areas. Perhaps the trend will reverse, and private practices will thrive.

Just in the past month, the dominant ophthalmology practice in our area, consisting of fifteen ophthalmologists, eighteen optometrists, two surgical centers, and eight locations, sold the business to a private equity firm. I am speculating that the owners, all of whom are ophthalmologists and getting closer to retirement age, realized that the chance of finding physicians willing to acquire the business was limited in this era where the future of health care is nebulous. Why not get their money out while they can?

Regulations such as the Stark Law limit how much a hospital system will pay for a practice or whether it will pay anything at all. To be fair, the complexities of practice management are significant and getting more difficult by the year. It's no wonder recent graduates defer from practicing independently; it takes a real entrepreneurial spirit to do otherwise. It's easier to join an established practice. If you really desire to be independent, consider specialties such as plastic surgery, ophthalmology, ENT, and dermatology. They are also some of the most competitive residencies to acquire. Could there be a correlation?

A medical practice requires equipment. This could mean as little as a few computers, examining room tables, and waiting room chairs, or you could have an ophthalmology practice with hundreds of thousands of dollars of sophisticated equipment. When you retire, even if no one is taking over the practice, that equipment is worth something. The cash generated could contribute to retirement savings.

I was fortunate both to be in a specialty that values private practice and that I could find someone to acquire my practice. While determining whether I could financially afford to retire, I analyzed the income that the sale of my practice would bring and its contribution to my entire retirement plan. My financial assets were borderline until I took into account the sale of my practice. An associate purchased my corporation, paying me for the practice, its equipment, and my accounts receivable. The transaction was made easier by self-financing, similar to a land contract on the sale of a home. I will receive a monthly check from my old practice for the next six years. We did not involve any financial institutions in the transaction, saving my associate the effort and expenses associated with a commercial loan.

I did not own an office building or a surgical center. Wouldn't it have been great if I had? Perhaps. Sometimes it's difficult to sell the practice, equipment, real estate, and surgical center at one time. Too large a financial burden may scare a buyer away. To reduce the initial purchase obligation, the original owner may keep ownership of the building, and the buyer may pay rent until the assets can be afforded. The original owner creates a stream of income for retirement either way.

My optical shops were not an independent business and as a result were sold as part of the practice. In other situations, they could be a separate entity. No matter which is the case, the sale of such assets generates money that can be contributed to a retirement fund. There are many business ventures in which an entrepreneurial physician can invest to enhance his or her practice's services and revenues. Sometimes they are part of a medical practice; often they are a separate entity. At retirement, the owner may want to sell all business interests or continue to retain ownership. If you have partners, it is possible by previous agreement that you will have to sell your interest in the related businesses once you are no longer partner in the original practice. No matter how the sale is organized, these assets can significantly augment retirement lifestyle.

Defined contribution (DC) and defined benefit (DB) programs are methods to save large amounts of money in pretax retirement accounts. They are generally not available to employed physicians and will be discussed in future chapters.

As you see, the sale of a practice can generate substantial income, from multiple sources. What better time to receive that money than at retirement? You may be paid in one lump sum or receive monthly payments over many years. Either way, the sale augments a formal retirement plan. Most new graduates, as employed physicians, will not have this opportunity when they retire. They will need to save consistently throughout their career via formal retirement plans and personal savings to get anywhere close to the assets required for a successful retirement. This may even require working an extra five to ten years.

4

"The Future Ain't What It Used to Be"

Forty years ago, many factory workers had generous retirement programs allowing them to retire after thirty years of employment, often with paid health care. Many were in their early fifties. Now employees in those same industries rely on self-financed 401(k) retirement programs and have no health care upon retirement. Wages have not kept up with inflation. Health insurance relies on large deductibles, and benefits are being squeezed. Self-employed physicians never had these benefits but rather depended on savings and sale of their business to fund themselves in retirement. This tradition is now threatened.

When you complete your residency and start earning a salary of $220,000 a year, you will be ecstatic. *Finally*, you will think, *a reward for my hard work! Time to reverse the deprivation!* But today's starting wages are a bit inflated. It is unlikely that you will produce enough income to cover your salary, benefits, and expenses in your first year or two of practice. My generation started at a lower salary, but we had a larger upside down the line. In the seventies and eighties, salaries were more reflective of the income you generated. Physicians often started their own practices. Take-home pay was income generated minus expenses.

If we didn't see many patients or had a high overhead, our take-home pay was marginal. My income for the first six months I was in practice was $14,000! But there was an upside. As we became busier, more efficient, and more effective, our incomes grew. We learned to manage our practices. Insurance companies increased their payments regularly.

Today you start with a higher salary. Why? Most employers are large practices or hospital corporations. They have deeper pockets. There is a bidding war, particularly for primary care. A competitive wage needs to be offered just to get your attention. Ever notice how some of the least desirable practices or locations offer the highest salaries? Administrators understand that if you stay somewhere for three years or so, you will be more likely to stay longer and put down roots. After about three years, your employer may shock you with a productivity contract.

When production isn't adequate, your income could be reduced the following year. The net result is that you may not earn significantly more as your practice matures. To complicate matters further, reimbursement from insurance companies has been flat for a decade and is not expected to grow significantly anytime in the future. Medicare's total growth has been capped at 0.5 percent annually until 2020 and then at 0 percent through 2025.[1] Commercial insurance companies usually follow Medicare's lead.

The only way to increase your income will be to see more patients and perform more procedures. Naturally, there is a limit to what you can do in a day, and this limit is exacerbated by the fact that your employer controls the staffing, scheduling, and purchasing of new equipment that you need to increase those volumes. It can be very difficult to convince "the man" that investments need to be made to increase your individual productivity. If you work for yourself or in a small group, this won't be a problem. You should be able to adjust. But if you are an employee of a large corporation, sustained effort may be necessary to get anything done. It will also take a great deal of time. Decisions that can be made quickly in your own practice may take months to years elsewhere.

If you listen to media or government, you're aware that physicians are often blamed for the high cost of health care. The public sees us as rich and entitled. Our profession is an easy mark for those trying to cut health-care costs. We cannot unionize and have weak representation in Congress. Our lobbyists compete poorly with those of the pharmaceutical and insurance industries. Hence, our reimbursement has been flat for the past decade and regulation rampant. When inflation is taken into consideration, our payments have declined. It is unlikely that the government or insurance will pay us more in the future.

Health care is eating away at larger and larger percentages of the American Gross Domestic Product (GDP). It is an expense that our government and industry would like to restrain. At the annual meeting of Berkshire Hathaway on May 6, 2017, Charles Munger, vice chairman of the company, said the following regarding health care:[2]

> If you go back to 1960, corporate taxes were about 4 percent of GDP, and now they are about 2 percent. In 1960, health care was 5 percent of GDP, and now it's about 17 percent of GDP. So when American business talks about taxes strangling our competitiveness, they are talking about something that as a percentage of GDP has gone down from 4 to 2 while medical costs, which are borne to a great extent by business, have gone from 5 to 17 percent. So medical costs are the tapeworm of American economic competitiveness.

During that same time period, health care costs in other countries have grown from 5 percent to 10 or 11 percent (*Ophthalmology Times* 42, no. 10 [June 15, 2017]: 4). It's clear that government and industry would prefer to restrain their spending on health care.

There are insurance programs that may increase your reimbursement if certain quality criteria are reported. But you also stand a chance of a reduction in your payments using those same criteria. According to the American Academy of Ophthalmology's "Academy Express," March 2017, the Centers for Medicare and Medicare Services reported that more than a third of US physicians were penalized effective January 1, 2017, for performance under their value-based modifier program, whereas only 1.4 percent received a bonus.[3] The bottom line is that it will be difficult for your salary to keep up with inflation. The only way to improve your take-home wage will be to increase productivity.

Drug companies routinely increase the cost of their products. You cannot do the same. Only a few physicians in specialties that provide services outside the scope of insurance will be able to adjust their charges. These include LASIK, plastic surgery, concierge, and infertility. But there is a limit to what they can charge due to market forces and the internet. In an effort to control payment for services, some physicians may decide not to accept insurance at all. Sounds great—charge what you feel your time is worth. But it's not as easy as you think. If you choose not to accept Medicare assignment for a patient's care, you cannot charge the patient more than 15 percent above what Part B of Medicare allows.[4] If you decide not to participate with Medicare at all, you are locked out for two years. You cannot decide to opt out of Medicare for one patient and not another. It's all or none.

Flat wages dictate that you cannot buy an expensive house and expect to grow into its payments. You cannot defer saving for retirement with the assumption that you'll have surplus money in the future to dedicate to it. Stretching out student loan payments twenty years will begin to interfere with investments in your children's education. Your home, auto, and other spending will need to be conservative because it is unlikely you will ever have higher wages to accommodate an over commitment. If you do overcommit, even tighter financial constraints will be needed to readjust.

When I was a general practitioner in the eighties, if I needed some extra spending money, I moonlighted, usually in an ER. That opportunity isn't likely to be available to you. The contract with your employer usually has a no-moonlighting covenant, and not just anyone can staff the ER anymore. Certainly, there are exceptions such as anesthesiologists picking up an extra call or ER docs taking additional shifts, but generally you will not be able to supplement your income by moonlighting. I expect flat wages to continue indefinitely.

During my years of practice, I was able to save enough money to support my family in retirement. In comparison to the computations I perform in the next chapters, where I use thirty-five years for retirement investments to accumulate, I was able to retire after twenty-six years because of my total dedication to retirement investing, owning my own practice, and my family's commitment to a moderate lifestyle. My success depended on all three components. Most new graduates will have complete access to only one of these conditions: the ability to live a modest lifestyle. Many of the formal retirement programs for tax-deferred saving will be unavailable, and few will have practice assets to sell. Attaining a comfortable retirement shall be a challenge!

Early on, I used an SEP-IRA. It was simple to use. All employees are required to receive an equal percentage of their salary in the plan. It became expensive as my practice grew. After finding a fee-only retirement advisor, I switched to a defined benefit plan (DB), where I was able to defer over $100,000 a year. Being older than my employees, I was able to retain a higher percentage of my income than my employees. Once I had an associate, I no longer participated in the DB plan due to its expense and switched to a defined contribution/profit-sharing plan. Although the deferrals were substantial, they did not come close to the amounts I had saved on the DB plan.

Sadly, as an employed physician, your opportunity to save with pretax contributions will be limited. You will likely never have the opportunity to participate in a defined benefit or profit-sharing plan but rather will depend on 401(k)/403(b) contributions and personal savings.

Regardless of which retirement plan you participate in, there is a significant tax benefit to deducting contributions while you are employed with income in a high tax bracket and then later, once retired, taking distributions in a lower tax bracket.

Retirement plans not only provide a tax break but also have asset-protection features. This is a complex issue that I am not qualified to address. Before you get involved with exotic offshore assets-protection plans, talk with your attorney about the benefits of a qualified retirement plan. Regulations frequently change and vary from state to state. In most states, a portion of your home value is also protected from creditors. Both situations, maximizing contributions to a qualified retirement plan and paying off your home mortgage, are easy ways to protect your assets.

5

401(k)/403(b) and Hospital Contributions

The most common retirement vehicle that large institutions use is either a 401(k) or a 403(b). 403(b) plans are used by government and nonprofits, 401(k) by private business. The income you receive upon retirement depends on your saving and investing within these plans. They work in essentially the same manner, allowing a tax-deferred contribution of up to $18,000 (as of 2017) a year.[1] Sometimes the institution will match some of your contribution, in addition to the $18,000 you invest yourself. Always take advantage of a match. It's free money! When you reach fifty, you are also allowed to put in an extra $6,000 (2017) a year in what is called a "catch-up." Some institutions will also have a 457 plan that allows another $18,000 contribution. Between the two you can contribute $36,000 a year!

I am going to begin a series of calculations, the purpose of which is to outline how much money needs to be saved for a successful retirement. They are as accurate as possible. You should review the calculations and make certain they apply to you.

Assuming you have access only to a 401(k) or 403(b) and you load it with the maximum $18,000 a year, starting at age thirty, how much money will you have at ages sixty-five, seventy, and seventy-five? Much depends on the rate of growth the money will achieve. Let's look at two fairly conservative growth rates, 5 percent and 7 percent (using the calculator at smartasset.com).

Retirement age	5% growth	7% growth
65	$1,802,420	$2,738,067
70	$2,436,516	$3,983,478
75	$3,245,937	$5,730,230

Two concepts are quickly evident. First, a higher rate of return results in much more money at retirement. Second, the longer you are invested, the greater your assets.

According to moneychimp.com the compounded average growth of the Standard & Poor's 500 Index (S&P 500) from January 1970 until December 2014 was 10.5 percent.[2] But the expansion for the ten years preceding December 2014 was only 7.94 percent. The highest growth rate since 1970 was 61 percent from June 1982 until June 1983. The lowest was minus 43 percent from March 2008 until March 2009. There are substantial short-term variations in the stock market, but over time growth averages out to a generous 10.5 percent. Hopefully, the next several decades of growth will be as generous. Since this number is an average, you need to be careful not to be too confident that your nest egg will be sufficient. To be safe, you should probably save more than you think you need. Imagine retiring in February 2008, thinking that you had enough saved for retirement, only to find a year later that your fund's value had decreased by 43 percent. When this occurred, many people had to delay their retirement and go back to work. I don't want this to happen to you.

Even though the stock market grew at 10.7 percent, don't expect your investments to do the same. Your investments should be dispersed into many categories both to take advantage of growth in varied financial products and to protect you from a sudden drop in the value of a single asset class. There are also costs involved with any investment. Low-cost investing should be your goal. It results in a higher net rate of growth in your investments. In evaluating the previous chart, it quickly becomes evident that a 2 percent smaller return in the 401(k)/403(b) results in almost a million-dollar difference after thirty-five years. It is common for physicians to be caught in investments with expenses of 2 percent or higher. Be vigilant. We will talk about this more later.

I used the conservative growth number of 7 percent in the earlier computations so that you get a realistic value. Imagine the disappointment and change in lifestyle you would need to make if you planned on your retirement funds earning 10 percent a year, and they made only 7 percent. A conservative prediction is always best. Having too much money is better than not having enough. Many states and municipalities are struggling with this very problem. The *Economist* reports that Dallas has a significant shortage of money in its employee retirement fund because the city "counted on an investment return of 8.5 percent a year, absurdly high in a world where the yield on ten-year treasury bonds has been hovering in the range of 1.5–3 percent." [3]

Our government wants everyone to have sufficient funds for retirement so as to prevent increased use of social services (tax dollars) and early use of Social Security. Consequently, there is a provision allowing for an extra $6,000 called a "catch-up" to be added to your 401(k)/403(b) yearly once you turn fifty years old. The government is aware that many people have not saved enough for retirement and need a little extra help. Be cautioned, though, that although helpful, catch-up contributions will not make up for not initiating a retirement savings plan well before you turn fifty. According to the bankrate.com retirement calculator, an additional $6,000 invested yearly starting at age fifty will grow to $117,592 at 5 percent growth and $135,303 at 7 percent by the age of sixty-five.

Starting at age 50
$6,000 yearly grows to:

	5%	7%
age 65	$117,592	$135,303

It is unlikely you will continue to contribute $6,000 past age sixty-five. If you do, the funds grow as follows:

age 70	$183,234	$224,274
age 75	$267,012	$349,060

This chart reinforces the need for you to give your investments time to grow. Start early, as soon as you begin to earn income, even in your residency. The additional $6,000 starting at age fifty, though helpful, will have modest effect on your retirement income and lifestyle and the decision of when to retire. But every bit helps. Take advantage of all the pretax opportunities possible.

After faithfully maximizing the investments in your 401(k)/403(b) for thirty-five years, including the catch-up, you will have now accumulated about $2,873,370 ($2,738,067 + $135,303) for retirement. William Bengen determined in the early nineties that a 4 percent yearly withdrawal from a retirement fund allowed it to continue regular payments for at least thirty years without loss of benefits.[4] Withdrawal of a greater percentage increases the chance that your retirement assets won't last thirty years. It is assumed that many of us will live into our nineties, so it is highly desirable that our retirement funds last that long. This 4 percent withdrawal rate has recently been called into question due to the current low-interest-rate environment. It's possible that retirement fund withdrawals in the future may need to be recalculated lower. Sadly, 4 percent of $2,873,370 is only about $115,000. Will you be able to live on that thirty-five years from now? Assuming a 3.2 percent inflation rate for the last century and extrapolating that to the future, $115,000 will be worth approximately $38,000 in today's money.

Remember how in chapter 2 my retirement fixed expenses were

$37,610? Once they were extrapolated to the year 2052, they became approximately $113,000, requiring about $2,825,000 in retirement assets. It's remarkable how close those computations come to the resources accumulated by maximizing 401(K)/403(B) contributions for thirty-five years.

It's clear that maximizing these retirement plans, though a desirable goal, will not provide enough income for a comfortable retirement lifestyle. It basically pays for barebones fixed expenses. How will you eat, pay for gasoline, take trips, and assist your grandchildren with college? More savings are required!

Hospitals and large corporations often contribute to their employees 401(k)/403(b) plans. It's called a match. It can be in addition to the $18,000 contribution from the individual employee. Recent inquiries to several hospitals' human resource departments indicate that these contributions average about $6,000 a year. According to the financial calculator at calculator.net, the value of this contribution in retirement at thirty-five, forty, and forty-five years, earning a 7 percent return, is as follows:

35 years	$829,421
40 years	$1,197,810
45 years	$1,714,495

If you are fortunate to receive a $6,000 match yearly, the $829,421 accumulated from employer matching at thirty-five years of employment can be added to the previously calculated $2,873,370 to produce a total retirement assets of $3,702,792. Living on 4 percent a year yields income of $148,112 per year, or $12,343 per month. Things are beginning to look better!

But this is $148,112 in 2052! How much is it in today's currency? Again, assuming an average inflation rate of 3.2 percent, it's worth about $50,000 today—similar to what you are making as a resident. Could you live on that? Do you want to try to live on that?

If you are a hospital employee, that may be all you can do to save pretax assets for retirement. It's obvious that more financial resources are needed. You will have to save them yourself, after taxes. The benefits of selling a practice won't exist for you.

There is one more retirement vehicle your hospital may have available to you. It is called a 457 plan. In this program, another 18,000 pretax dollars may be saved. It's a little quirky, and many hospitals don't emphasize it. One I spoke with had only six participants among its hundreds of physicians. There are two types of 457 plans, governmental and nongovernmental. In the governmental plan, if you leave employment at that institution, the money can be rolled into an IRA. With the nongovernmental program, when you leave employment, the funds may not be rolled into another tax-deferred retirement plan other than another nongovernmental 457 plan. This may not be possible, prompting dispersal of the assets and taxes.[5] Many physicians avoid investing in nongovernmental 457 plans.

If you maximize investment in the 457 along with an $18,000 401(k)/403(b) contribution, the hospital gift of $6,000, and a catch-up, what is your retirement nest egg after thirty-five years? Assuming 7 percent growth, it's about $6,440,859. Is that enough to provide a comfortable retirement starting in 2052? Returning to Bengen's 4 percent hypothesis, $257,600 annually could safely be removed for living expenses. With an inflation rate of 3.2 percent, that would be worth about $85,000 today. Could you live on this at age sixty-five?

Don't forget—you should also receive some assistance from Social Security (SS). How much? Who knows. Will it continue to exist for high-wage earners? Will you be considered a high-wage earner? Today, in 2017, the top payment for which you would qualify after earning $220,000 a year is $32,244. There is an inflation equation built into payments. Hopefully, it will keep up with actual inflation. But don't count on it. Our government is manipulating SS payments to assist in its survival. Last year, benefits rose only 0.3 percent, whereas inflation rose 2.1 percent.[6] It's impossible to predict the value of Social Security payments in 2052. Let's hope you receive a payment at least equal to the value today. Adding SS to $85,000, we reach a new retirement value of $117,244 in 2017 dollars. In reality, perhaps only 50 to 75 percent of the current SS benefit will be available to you in 2052. A more realistic number is $106,281 (two-thirds of SS—$21,281—plus $85,000). Looking better! You could probably live in retirement with this income, although you might need to make a lifestyle adjustment.

Few physicians are taking advantage of or have access to 457 plans. The extra $18,000 a year invested in them gets you into the low end of the comfort zone for retirement. If you don't have a 457 option, you need to save at least $18,000 per year yourself for a marginally comfortable retirement (in addition to maximized 402(k)/403(b), catch-up, and hospital contributions).

Several other retirement plans exist. Both the Roth IRA and traditional IRA can be used in addition to an employer-sponsored retirement plan. The time to use these may be while you are a resident with modest income. Once you earn $118,000 (2017) for married filing jointly, use of the traditional IRA disappears. You can earn up to $196,000 (2017), married filing jointly, and still participate in a Roth IRA.[7] This is a great program because your after-tax contributions grow tax-free, but your ability to contribute is limited by your financial success.

In summary, as an employed physician, it's unlikely you will have enough saved to retire comfortably without making extraordinary efforts. About $44,000 needs to invested yearly for thirty years you to have a modest retirement. It is important to maximize all retirement programs through your employer, but you will still need to save considerably more on your own in after-tax vehicles. This will require living a modest lifestyle. Be prepared to work past age sixty-five for both the extra income and the increase in your assets that occur over time.

6

Defined Contributions

Defined contribution (DC) plans are a very useful mechanism to save for retirement pretax and are used in addition to other plans such as a 401(k). The income you receive upon retirement depends on your own saving and investment. Contribution is by the employee only and can be up to the lesser of 25 percent of compensation or $54,000 (2017).[1] This limit includes the $18,000 from a 401(k) and any form of employer contribution. Remember the $6,000 mentioned earlier? It's possible that as an employee of a large group or institution, you may receive a small contribution, but it's unlikely to be anywhere near the maximum possible contribution. These plans are most available when you are self-employed or in a small group. In those situations, you are able to decide with your partners the amount you would like to place in the plan. Hopefully, you can max it out. A catch-up of $6,000 is also allowed in these programs, so once you are fifty years old, $60,000 (2017) can be tax-deferred.

A similar amount, $54,000, may be deferred in a SEP-IRA.[2] This plan is also used by self-employed physicians. It is often costlier than a DC plan because all full-time employees must receive the same percentage of their income as you contribute to yours. In other words, if you place 20 percent of your income in the SEP, you must place the same percentage for all your employees. This may not be a problem with only one or two employees, but costs can escalate quickly with large staffs. DC plans allow a larger percentage of income to be deferred for highly compensated employees, saving the practice money.

As a self-employed physician, I participated in a defined contribution program for years. It worked well for me. Let's see how it will affect your retirement. Again, if you start at age thirty and work until age sixty-five while maximizing a contribution of $54,000 and a rate of return of 7 percent, the lump sum at age sixty-five would be about $7,987,326.83 (financial calculator at calculator.net). Now we're talking real money. Add in the catch-up provision of $6,000 per year ($135,303) starting at age fifty, and the total sum becomes $8,122,629.

Could you live comfortably on this amount for thirty years? Four percent of $8,122,629 is about $325,000. That sounds like a fantastic retirement income. But wait, I am talking 2052 dollars! Let's see what that amount would be worth in today's terms. That should give us an idea of whether you will have saved enough. Using an average inflation rate of 3.2 percent, the present value would be about $108,000. Add in two-thirds of the current Social Security benefit (I am assuming SS benefits will decline over the next thirty-five years by a third in real value), $22,281, and you'll be surviving on $129,281. Let's round it to $130,000. Is that enough to sustain your robust $220,000-per-year standard of living?

When you earn $220,000, are you really living the equivalent lifestyle? Subtract the $54,000 you are putting into your retirement plan. You are now living at the $166,000 level. School loan payments of $30,000 per year reduce net spendable income to $136,000. It appears that the income derived from a fully funded defined contribution plan will return a very familiar lifestyle. You should be able to live on that in retirement. By 2052, you shouldn't have school or mortgage debt. Your children will be grown. Your cars will be paid off. My income in retirement is similar to this, and I am not suffering from any financial strain. As a disclaimer, I live in a small town in the Midwest and have a modest lifestyle except for travel. If I can do it, you can too!

It appears that if you are able to save the maximum allowed defined contribution of $54,000 a year for thirty-five years, maximize the catch-up for another fifteen years, and receive Social Security payments, you should have a successful retirement. It won't be lavish, but it will be comfortable. Any additional money saved past this point will make retirement more comfortable and reliable.

Bottom line: You will need about $8,000,000 to retire comfortably thirty-five years from now.

7

Worst-Case Scenarios

I recently had a discussion with a financial advisor friend of mine. He is concerned that returns in the stock market will be reduced over the next several decades, and he wants me to be certain to show you the retirement income derived from a lower growth rate. He feels that the market is overbought and that our economy is growing slowly. Considering these issues, let's determine the value of your retirement resources if the market were to grow at only 5 percent rather than the 7 percent we calculated earlier.

Contributing the maximum $54,000 yearly for thirty-five years, adding in the catch-up at age fifty, and allowing it all to grow at 5 percent results in approximately $5,240,000. Four percent of that is about $210,000. At present values, assuming 3.2 percent inflation, that income would be roughly $70,000 a year. To continue this "worst-case" scenario, let's assume that Social Security doesn't grow commensurate with inflation and that its value thirty-five years from now is only two-thirds what it is today. With the addition of $21,281 (0.66 x $32,244) from SS, the net present value of retirement income becomes approximately $91,000. You could live on this amount, perhaps not as comfortably as you wish, but hopefully, your mortgage and school loans would be paid off, and your children would be out of the home.

Taking the "worst case" one step further, let's continue to assume that the return of your investments is only 5 percent but that instead of retiring after thirty-five years, you are forced to retire after only twenty-five years due to poor health. Your retirement savings are all you have to live on. Investing $54,000 a year for twenty-five years with a 5 percent return results in approximately $2,700,000. Living off only 4 percent or less becomes very important because you may need these assets longer than our previous assumption of thirty years. Therefore, $108,000 will be available to live on twenty-five years from now, present value being about $49,000. Adding SS of $21,281 results in about $70,000 a year to live on in 2017 dollars.

If you were able to save only $36,000 a year for twenty-five years while earning 5 percent, the total saved would be $1,804,084. Withdrawing 4 percent would allow you to live on $72,163 starting in 2042. In today's money that would be about $33,000. Adding in the reduced SS benefits, the total retirement income in 2042 becomes about $55,570. That could be a struggle.

In another scenario, you are employed by a hospital system and can save only $18,000 in a 403(b). You have no other savings, and health concerns force you to retire at age fifty-five after twenty-five years of investments. A poor stock market environment allows growth of only 5 percent. Thus, total retirement assets are about $860,000. Four percent withdrawal allows you $34,400, which is the equivalent of $16,500 today. Adding in the reduced SS value of $21,281, the present value of income would be about $38,000. It would be very difficult to survive on this income in retirement!

Bengen's calculation of 4 percent withdrawal takes into account the fluctuations of the market. Withdrawal of this amount should allow the original principal to last at least thirty years. It's calculated for good and bad times. In periods of good economic growth, the principal may last longer. Perhaps you don't want to leave millions to your heirs upon your death. Should you leave half your retirement assets, a quarter, or nothing at your death? It's clearly an individual choice. It's difficult to plan on leaving nothing because you may run out of assets before you die. If you have saved successfully, you will probably be able to live comfortably in retirement and still bequeath a substantial amount to your heirs. But should economic growth stumble prior to and during the early years of your retirement, you may spend down your resources quicker, leaving less. There is a fine line between retaining 50 percent of your resources and having nothing left after thirty years of retirement. A close eye will need to be kept later in retirement to ensure you do not run out of money.

The Japanese stock market Nikkei Index was almost 40,000 in 1989. A recession beginning in that year reduced the Nikkei to the level of 15,000 by 1992 and to less than 10,000 by September 2001.[1] It has gradually risen since then but was only 19,979 on June 6, 2017.[2] It retains only 50 percent of its value twenty-eight years later! Imagine this decline happening to your investments shortly before you retire or, even worse, ten years into your retirement. Although a decline of this degree, for this long, has never happened in the United States, that doesn't mean that such a recession cannot occur. This is a very strong reason to maximize your retirement savings, diversify your investments, and live a modest lifestyle. Hopefully, if the US stock market declines, alternative investments will provide some stability in your portfolio. Perhaps you will have to work a few extra years.

Let's imagine that a Japanese-like economic downturn occurs shortly after your retirement. You lose 50 percent of your retirement savings, and there is no growth in the market for decades. At age sixty-five your fully funded 401(k)/403(b) of $2,873,370 now becomes $1,436,685. A Bengen 4 percent withdrawal is $57,467, the current value of which is about $19,500. Adding a discounted SS of $21,281 results in a yearly income of about $41,000 in today's dollars. But market growth is flat! There will be no growth of your portfolio. If $57,467 is removed annually, your retirement assets will disappear in twenty-five years.

But it's likely you would need to remove resources at a higher rate to survive. Suppose you remove twice the Bengen 4 percent, approximately $115,000. The current value would be about $39,000, and when this is combined with a discounted SS, your income would reach around $60,000. Although it would be much easier to survive financially on this amount, life still would have to be very frugal, and the principal would last only about twelve years. At age seventy-seven, you would be broke. How would you make adjustments?

In a similar scenario with a fully funded DC plan of $8,122,629, half is lost due to a market crash, and there is no growth for several decades. A 4 percent yearly withdrawal plus discounted SS would result in an income of approximately $75,000 in today's dollars. Since $75,000 a year might not be enough to maintain your desired lifestyle, let's see what happens when 6 percent is removed annually. With the larger amount of principal saved in a DC plan, you may feel more comfortable taking the extra amount. Six percent withdrawal would result in income of $244,000 a year—about $81,000 in 2017 currency. Adding a discounted SS contribution would result in your having approximately $102,000 to live on. Although this is a much more comfortable lifestyle, your money will run out in sixteen years, when you are age eighty-one.

An infinite number of situations can be considered. I have reviewed only a few. If you want to play with the numbers, place them in a calculator such as the financial calculator at calculator.net. See what you get. Basically, the more money you save, the greater your chance of having a comfortable retirement. Very simple. We cannot predict the future, so we need to be prepared for a wide range of contingencies.

8

Working Longer

If you live in the Northeast or on the West Coast, the income derived from maximizing savings in a defined contribution will not be enough for a comfortable retirement. If you have a moderately high lifestyle, your assets will be insufficient. If you are used to living the high life and figure that at retirement you will suddenly switch to a modest lifestyle, don't fool yourself. Can't live on the equivalent of $220,000 a year in 2052? Something has to change. Now that you understand the need for extensive retirement savings, you will spend less, save more, and/or work longer to reach the goal. Worst-case scenario: you ignore the warning and run out of money. Do you like Ramen Noodles?

If you decide to work longer, past age sixty-five, should you keep contributing to a retirement plan? How much money would you have at retirement if you didn't touch the principal you had acquired by age sixty-five and let it grow in the market for ten more years at 7 percent interest while you continued to work? The previously calculated $8,816,747 you have accumulated by maximizing your defined contribution and catch-up becomes about $17,343,875. That's a lot of money, or so it seems. Remember, we are calculating for forty-five years in the future. You will

41

be seventy-five years old and probably won't live more than another twenty years. The 4 percent yearly withdrawal to preserve assets for thirty years goes out the window. You could easily withdraw a million dollars a year without fear your assets will disappear before you do. A million dollars in 2062 is estimated to be worth $250,000 in today's money.

Unless you are exceedingly disciplined not only in saving for retirement but also in maintaining a modest lifestyle, you are going to need to work past age sixty-five. Will you need to work until age seventy-five? I cannot say. It depends on your living expenses, savings, health, and multiple other factors.

To simplify things, the computations in this book are for a family with one wage earner. If you have a spouse who also contributes to retirement savings and SS, you will achieve your goals more easily. But both of you combined will still need to save a total of at least $54,000 a year plus the catch-up and SS for a modest retirement. Everything saved after that is icing on the cake.

Whether your spouse is employed or not, the fastest way to lose both post-tax and pretax retirement assets is to become divorced. The damage is most dramatic in a single-wage-earner family. Dividing assets in half can set back retirement planning a decade or more. Perhaps the greatest challenge to becoming a millionaire is getting divorced.

Every year the federal government recalibrates the amount of money that may be tax- deferred in formal retirement plans. The current maximum of $54,000 in defined contribution will gradually increase, as will the $18,000 in a 401(k)/403(b). If you consistently maximize contributions to your retirement plan, the resulting totals will be larger than our calculations. How much larger?

The allowed deferral in 1997 for a 401(k) was $9,500 and for DC was $30,000.[1] The growth of these allocations has averaged about 3.0 percent over the past twenty years, reaching the current levels of $18,000 and $54,000. It's great that our government is increasing our allowed contributions by the rate of inflation! If that growth rate is extrapolated into the future, by 2052 the allowed contributions should be about

$50,500 for 401(k)/403(b) and $152,000 for a defined contribution. Continuing to maximize contributions over this time period results in a retirement nest egg that is about 27 percent larger. A 401(k)/403(b) will be worth around $3,500,000, and a defined contribution about $10,300,000. These calculations have not included the catch-up or employer contribution. But growing the catch-up by 3 percent yearly for fifteen years adds only marginally to these large figures.

My hypothesis is that salaries for physicians in the future will be stagnant. If this is the case, at some point it will be impossible to dedicate the increasing allowable contributions to your DC. It will be hard to contribute $152,000 when your total income is $200,000 or even $300,000. But please, try to contribute as much as possible, as soon as possible and for as long as possible. It is impossible to know how much you will need, when you will need it, or whether there will there be a significant downturn in the market. We have already determined that you should be able to have a comfortable retirement by saving $54,000 a year for thirty-five years, barring any unforeseen complications.

As an employed physician with only a 401(k)/403(b), you will definitely need to maximize your contributions as the allowable amount increases yearly. You should be able to afford them. But this will yield only approximately $3,500,000. Achieving the retirement comfort level of $8,000,000 will require additional savings of $4,500,000 on your own, in an after-tax account.

There is a tax-deferred retirement plan in which huge amounts of money can be saved. It is called a defined benefit program.[2] It is a complex and expensive way to creatively accrue large sums of tax-free money over a short period of time. It is unlikely you will be able to take advantage of one unless you are self-employed or in a very small group where all members have similar financial goals. It requires actuarial certification yearly and is often used by self-employed physicians late in their career to accumulate retirement funds. Literally hundreds of thousands of dollars a year can be allocated pretax to retirement—a phenomenal opportunity if you qualify.

9

High Costs of Living

Those of you who live in areas with a high cost of living have a herculean task ahead of you. It will be difficult for physicians living in moderately expensive locations to save enough to retire comfortably. To retire with a similar lifestyle in a high-cost location will be almost impossible. The cost of living calculator at bankrate.com states that the cost of living in Brooklyn, New York, is 87.45 percent higher than in Grand Rapids, Michigan.[1] Numbeo.com lists the difference at about 80 percent.[2] But this doesn't tell the whole story. Median price of a home in Grand Rapids is $244,000, whereas in Brooklyn it is $963,000.[1] Essentially, retirement savings will need to be almost double the $8,000,000 value calculated earlier, or about $16,000,000 plus Social Security.

Don't give up! You certainly should continue to maximize your retirement savings. ($54,000, catch-up, and SS). Again, if you are not self-employed, most of the savings for retirement will have to come from post-tax dollars. Maximize your working spouse's contributions too. Look closely at your standard of living. Can it be reduced? Avoid unnecessary debt. Make a budget.

If your spouse is a professional with a similar income, depending on employment situations, each of you could contribute $54,000 into a DC. This should be enough to satisfy your retirement dreams.

Perhaps the most important consideration of all is whether to move to an area with a lower cost of living. Do you do this now at the beginning of your career or after retirement? Lots of decisions to make. Florida and Texas are looking better all the time.

10

Wages after Inflation

I previously discussed the evidence suggesting that physicians' wages will not rise substantially in the future. Income certainly will not keep up with inflation, which has averaged 3.2 percent over many decades. Assuming a modest growth of 2 percent a year in wages, an initial salary of $220,000 will grow to approximately $440,000 (calculator.net) a year in thirty-five years. Your purchasing power will be less than when you first went into practice. Continuing a similar lifestyle in retirement will require savings of around $11,000,000.

How much will your starting salary of $220,000 a year be worth in thirty-five years if it does grow at 3.2 percent? About $660,000! Unless you earn $660,000 a year when you retire, your buying power will be less than when you finished residency. Scary! To withdraw 4 percent after retirement and maintain this lifestyle, you will require a nest egg of about $16,500,000.

A simple way of determining your lump-sum retirement assets requirement is to multiply the income you desire by twenty-five. In this example, $440,000 times twenty-five equals the $11,000,000 mentioned previously. If you have maximized contributions to a 401(k)/403(b) and have participated in the catch-up, you will have about three million dollars in retirement savings. An additional $8,000,000 will be needed to properly fund that $440,000 lifestyle in 2052 (a lifestyle that is about $140,000 in 2017 dollars).

As an employed physician with limited retirement plan options and no practice assets to sell, you will require significant additional retirement savings and lifestyle modifications. Accumulating a large amount of money outside of a retirement account is difficult. Without significant discipline the tendency will be to spend it: "I have enough money to buy that new car." "We can afford that trip." "A million-dollar house, no problem. We have plenty for the down payment." Try to keep retirement investments separated from your normal day-to-day money, perhaps in a different bank or in an investment account that is well marked with its intentions. The moment you start dipping into it, your discipline may falter. Your savings will disappear. It is not only you who needs to be disciplined but also your spouse. You both need to be on the same page, or you'll fail. Consider this mantra: "Because I value my freedom I exercise the financial discipline to maintain that freedom"[1]

There is value to having savings on which the taxes already have been paid. It allows you in retirement to blend income from retirement funds and private savings to adjust your tax rate. By using the cash in your post-tax investment account, you reduce the need for withdrawals from a retirement plan on which income taxes will need to be paid. Your non-retirement investment savings have already been taxed, so when you spend them, you are responsible for paying taxes only on the growth of the money, not its principal. This tax rate may be lower if the growth comes from dividends or capital gains (rates of 0 percent to 20 percent compared with 10 percent to 39.6 percent on regular income).[2]

You and your spouse are the only ones who can determine the lifestyle you want to live before and after retirement. Those decisions will decide how much money is available for retirement savings. Use the calculations provided previously to assist you in those evaluations.

Sometimes you may ask yourselves, "Are we saving money so that someday we can have a life and by doing that delaying having a life now?" Hopefully, careful planning and the use of time to grow your assets will allow you to live well before and after retirement.

11

Health Savings Accounts

A health savings account (HSA) is a tax-advantaged medical savings account associated with a high-deductible health plan. Since being signed into law by President George W. Bush on December 8, 2003, it has become a popular health insurance option. Up to $3,400 per person and $6,750 per family (as of 2017) can be placed into an account. An additional $1,000 is allowed for those over fifty-five years of age. Contributions are pretax, and the money grows tax-deferred. It's another way to reduce your taxable income and grow assets tax-deferred.[1]

If not used, contributions roll over from year to year and accumulate. Funds can be used for any qualified medical expense. HSAs encourage saving for future health-care outlays. It's felt that these plans help make consumers more responsible for their own care.

I have had an HSA for many years. Currently, its balance is over $29,000. It was last used to pay for a prescription copay and before that a dental procedure. I no longer need to get dental or optical insurance since these items are being paid for with my HSA. Once I enroll in Medicare next year, I will no longer be able to contribute but will still be able to use the HSA's assets to pay for medical expenses. HSA funds can even be used to pay for Medicare premiums, deductibles, and copays.

Not all employers have an option for this plan. If available, it certainly bears consideration.

12

Investing 101

Disclaimer: I am not a financial advisor. The ideas in this chapter are discussed to better familiarize you with aspects of financial planning and to help you make better decisions. It has taken me years and many mistakes to learn these subjects, and I am still learning. Do your own research before you invest, and always consider consultation with a certified financial planner—preferably one who is fee-based and a fiduciary.

It seems very simplistic, but the most important concept in investing is that you should start saving money now! If you don't save any money, there's nothing to invest! If you don't invest, how will assets grow? If you don't have any financial resources, how will you retire? We previously showed how you will need about $8,000,000 for a successful retirement thirty-five years from now. Money doesn't appear overnight. It's impossible to accumulate that much over the last ten years of your practice. It takes an entire career—decades! How do you save money? It takes a plan and discipline. But it really isn't that hard. I did it! Why am I encouraging you to save money—lots of money? Because I want you to be able to retire someday. I don't want you to have to work until you are eighty-five or live on peanut butter and jelly sandwiches in subsidized housing because you haven't saved.

It is important to start investing for retirement as soon as possible, preferably while you are a resident. Many residency programs allow you to participate in their institutional retirement plans. They may also match you with some free money! Take advantage! How often are you given free money? If a plan is not available, open up an IRA on your own. If you don't have the resources, moonlight. To illustrate the importance of saving early and utilizing the value of compounding growth, let's look at two scenarios.

First, how much money would you have in your retirement account at age sixty-five if you contributed only from age thirty until forty and then never invested a cent again, saving for only ten years but doing it early? Compare this value to starting late at age forty but continuing contributions until age sixty-five—a quarter of a century of savings but starting late. Twenty-five years of contributions should build a larger portfolio than ten, shouldn't it?

Assuming that a maximized defined contribution (DC) of $54,000 is saved yearly from age thirty until forty, with no further contributions and 7 percent compounding growth, $4,049,343 will be present at age sixty-five: about half of the value you would have by saving the maximum in your DC for thirty-five years.

Contributing the same $54,000 a year but starting a decade later at age forty, continuing until age sixty-five while receiving 7 percent growth, will result in a balance of $3,415,448: a difference of $633,895!

Clearly, starting early is extremely important if you want to get to the approximately $8,000,000 you will need for a successful retirement. But you cannot stop saving after only ten years, or you will have accumulated only half of what you need for a successful retirement.

Many financial instruments exist to assist you in saving. We have already discussed the 401(k)/403(b) and 457 plans and the defined contribution and defined benefit programs. They are of no help unless you take advantage of them. If you want a comfortable retirement, you need to stuff these plans with the most money possible. If your defined contribution plan is maximized ($54,000/year in 2017), as discussed in chapter 6, you will likely have the roughly $8,000,000 you'll need for a successful retirement. As you know, many of these programs are not available to "employed" physicians. In that case, physicians will need to maximize the plans available to them and make up the difference on their own. This means after-tax saving and investing. This is the part that really requires planning and self-control. If you don't start early, contribute regularly, and avoid spending this money on other things, you will have insufficient funds to retire.

The second important investing concept is that money needs time to grow. The more time, the more money. The growth of assets (interest, dividends) in a retirement account is added to the principal, so that subsequent growth is based on the larger value. Think of it as earning interest on interest. This is called compounding and allows your retirement resources to grow exponentially with time. As I illustrated in chapter 5, an additional five or ten years of growth allows investments to grow significantly. This is critical for young physicians. Compared to your non-physician peers, your years of training have taken you out of the job market and prevented you from saving for retirement for almost a decade. You need to start saving as soon as possible, or you won't get the growth that time generates.

To illustrate this concept further, consider the parlor trick where you are asked whether you would rather have a million dollars or the amount of money that would exist if you doubled the value of a penny for a month. In your head, you start doing the math: 1, 2, 4, 8, 16 ... After ten steps, the value is only $5.12. There is no way this could result in more than a million dollars! But it does. At twenty days, the value is $5,242.88. By day twenty-five, it is $167,772.16. On day thirty it suddenly balloons to $5,368,709.12. During the last five days, the values climb exponentially. This is similar to what I want to happen to your money! To start to get some real growth, you need to leave it invested for more than twenty-five years.

Several quotes regarding compound interest are attributed to Albert Einstein. He is reputed to have said that it is "the most powerful force of the universe," and he also called it the "greatest invention in human history." [1] Although this may be hyperbole, it is certainly a significant force that you want on your side.

It seems that if you are investing $54,000 a year in a retirement savings program with a 7 percent growth rate, your money should grow rapidly. But similar to the penny trick mentioned previously, the growth of assets is very small until about twenty-five years, when it becomes exponential. Seven percent of $54,000 is only $3,780. It takes a lot of instances of $3,780 compounded to accumulate any substantial growth. Have your money invested long-term so that you can benefit from the growth curve going exponential.

The last critical investing concept is maximizing your rate of return on investments. The stock market grows at a rate that varies from day to day, but over the last one hundred years that rate has averaged about 10 percent. [2] Your investments will not average anywhere close to that number for several reasons. They will not be 100 percent in stocks but rather will be in a mixture of investments including bonds, real estate, and other assets. This concept, called diversification, protects your investments from radical losses during downturns in the market. It also tends to lower your average return. All investments also have a cost associated with them. These costs are subtracted from the return, resulting in lower growth. Lower costs result in a higher rate of return.

13

Improving Investment Returns

To maximize your rate of return, you need consistent high growth as well as low cost. For example, if your investment is returning 7 percent a year but costs 3 percent to administer, your net return is only 4 percent.

To grow your assets most efficiently, it's important to avoid investments with high costs. The chart in chapter 6 illustrated the difference in asset growth between 401(k)/403(b) plans that had a return of 5 percent and 7 percent. Over thirty-five years the difference is greater than $900,000! This 2 percent difference can be achieved by simply minimizing the costs associated with investing. All investments have a cost or expense associated with them. It takes work to manage your investments. Your managers will want to be paid. The secret is to pay the least you can. The more people who handle your money, the increased likelihood expenses will be high. Everyone wants a piece of the action, and they will nickel-and-dime you.

A mutual fund is a pool of money from a large group of investors that purchases different securities. Funds exist for many types of investments. Costs associated with them are called loads and are charged as a percentage of the fund you are buying or selling. Four types of mutual funds exist in regard to their loads:[1]

- Front-loaded funds require a commission fee at the time of purchase.
- Back-loaded funds demand a commission fee when they are sold.
- Constant-load funds receive commission fees at regular intervals.
- No-load funds do not pay commission.

No-load funds are the only type the average investor should purchase. Scrutinize all your investments. If you are using a broker or insurance person as an investment advisor, there is a high probability that person will get you into a loaded or high-expense fund, reducing your return.

The reason generally given to encourage you to buy into a loaded fund is that you are paying for the expertise of the "money manager." Advisors suggest that if you receive this expertise, your investments will grow better than if they were in a no-load or minimally guided fund. This concept was generally disproved during the 1970s in multiple articles by Paul Samuelson, Al Ehrbar, and Charles Ellis.[2] In 1975 John Bogle started the First Index Investment Trust for individual investors.[3] Now called the Vanguard 500 Index Fund, it tracks the S&P 500 and initiated access to low-cost investments for the public. Availability of funds such as this allowed my peers and me to have access to quality low-cost investments—an opportunity that previous generations of investors didn't have. Certainly, there are years when the loaded fund will do better than an index fund, but there are also times when it does worse. Generally, over time most investment returns achieve the average of the market. If you are in a loaded fund that over time returns the same growth as a non-loaded fund, you actually are losing money. Remember that 1 or 2 percent load you paid? Some funds have a 5.75 percent charge!

Exchange-traded funds (ETFs) are marketable securities that track an index, a commodity, bonds, or a basket of assets such as an index fund. Unlike a mutual fund, an ETF trades like a common stock. Price can vary throughout the day. Capital gains realized inside the fund are not passed directly through to the shareholder.[4] They are generally not actively managed. Their low-cost, stock-like trading features, tax efficiency, and diversification make them an attractive investment vehicle. Expenses may be 90 percent cheaper than retail mutual funds. [5]

In addition to loads, there are costs associated with all funds. They are called expenses and reported as the expense ratio. The expense ratio represents the percentage of the fund's assets that go toward managing the fund. At the end of the year, that percentage is subtracted from the return the fund achieved. It is that lower number you receive as an investor. The average expense for an actively managed fund is about 1.5 percent. This percentage is removed from your account whether it's been a good or bad year. Some mutual fund families try to keep their expenses ratios as low as possible. Vanguard is well known for low-cost investments, and its funds average expense ratio is 0.12 percent. [6] The Financial Industry Regulatory Authority (FINRA) has a website, apps. finra.org, that lists data on all mutual funds and ETFs. Using it, I found that the Vanguard S&P 500 Index Fund has an expense ratio of 0.16 percent. It reports that the 301 funds of comparable peers have an average expense of 1.29 percent. It's possible to save or rather make an extra 1 percent a year just by concentrating on expense ratios.

You have just learned two concepts that could make you a million dollars! Remember how the difference between a 5 percent and 7 percent return on your 401(k)/403(b) was $900,000? Well, avoid loaded funds, and you save at least 1 percent. Use low-cost funds and save up to another 1 percent. Voila! Two percent better return on your investments. Almost a million bucks! It isn't hard work, and it doesn't require a great deal of knowledge. You just need to pay attention. This is where you see the savings associated with a fee-based advisor. He or she may charge you a few thousand dollars a year for advice, but the broker/ insurance representative can cost you millions!

In 2011 AARP asked workers throughout the country how many had fees associated with their retirement plan. Seventy-one percent mistakenly said they paid none.[7] All investments have fees associated with them; it's just that they are not obvious. They are probably not on your statement. Could you imagine getting a mortgage and not knowing the interest rate? These costs are hidden because your advisor doesn't want you to know the true cost of your investment. Some of this money is going to him or her instead of to growing your portfolio. The average actively managed fund has an expense ratio of 1.5 percent. That doesn't seem so bad until you realize that such funds also average 1.44 percent annually in trading expenses. If the market averages 9 percent growth yearly, the real growth of an average retail mutual fund will be only 6.06 percent. You are losing almost a third of your profits yearly. Expenses have real effects!

Most physicians don't have the time or interest to manage their own money. There are thousands of financial professionals whose business is to transfer money from your pocket to theirs. The difficult part is determining whom you can trust. The first "financial advisor" most individuals come in contact with is an insurance person. I hate to generalize, but insurance providers don't have a good track record for investing in your interest. I am not saying all are not to be trusted, but be very wary. Once a bond is formed, you may be taken into some investments you later regret. It takes a great effort to get a second opinion or switch advisors. Most individuals stay with their first "advisor" and pay the penalty. If you wait ten to fifteen years before you switch to a low-cost advisor, you will have lost significant growth in your portfolio. It's never too late or too early for a second opinion.

Investing is complicated and can be expensive with the wrong investment advisor. It is recommended that you consult a certified financial advisor, preferably one who charges you a flat fee and doesn't benefit from each product sold to you. Consider a fiduciary. Be cautious with salespeople such as stockbrokers and insurance representatives.

Most of my investments are managed by a nationally known bank trust department. All bank trust departments are fiduciaries. As a fiduciary, advisors must act in the best interests of their clients, and to put their clients' interests above their own. It leaves no room for advisors to conceal any potential conflict of interest, and requires that all fees and commissions must be clearly disclosed to clients.[8] Up until now most insurance agents and stockbrokers were not fiduciaries. They followed a looser regulation called the Suitability Rule, which meant that as long as an investment met the client's general "needs and objectives," it was considered appropriate. The Department of Labor has issued new regulations, effective April 10, 2017. These rules require all financial advisors, including insurance agents and stockbrokers, to become fiduciaries when dealing with retirement accounts. This wasn't a popular move in some circles, and President Trump issued a 180-day delay in implementation on February 3, 2017. In early August, 2017, the Department of Labor filed a court document as part of a lawsuit in the U.S. District Court for the District of Minnesota, proposing an 18-month delay to the rule's compliance.[9] Not covered in this new fiduciary rule are after-tax accounts earmarked for retirement but not actually in formal plans. Additionally excluded are specific retirement investments for which the customer directly asks. Whether or not this plan goes into effect, investors will still need to be vigilant. Some say that the fiduciary rule won't make a difference since "crooks" will just hide their scams in reams of paper. There is great concern in the insurance industry, for if the new rule goes into effect, insurance agents will need to disclose commissions and costs associated with financial investments and likely will lose the income derived from selling them. Commissions generated by selling annuities and whole life are quite substantial. The brokerage sections of MetLife and American International Group have already been sold in anticipation of the decreased sales and increased costs the new rule will bring about.[10] .

Most bank trust departments don't accept clients unless they have significant financial assets to invest. Some smaller banks may require only a quarter of a million dollars, whereas the more prestigious, larger institutions require millions. It takes a minimum of two million dollars to be managed at the institution where I bank. The management fee is a flat percentage of the dollars invested. The more money you have, the less you pay. The first two million dollars cost 1.00 percent; the next three million, 0.75 percent; and another five million, 0.55 percent. By the time your assets are greater than twenty-five million, management costs are only 0.25 percent. Upon investigation, I have found an institution, Isabella Bank Trust Services of Mt. Pleasant, Michigan, that does not have a minimum investment account requirement. The bank charges a flat 1 percent management fee and is willing to negotiate the fee lower in the case of a large account. Minimum investment fee is $2,000. Until you accumulate $200,000, your management fee shall be greater than 1 percent.[11] That may not be unreasonable. The trust is less likely to place you in the expensive investments that brokers or insurance salespeople use, saving you money in the long run.

Beware of the syndrome of "My advisor is such a nice person; he/she would never take advantage of me." Yes, advisors will! That's their job. Unless they are certified fiduciaries, those smiles and free lunches are there to sell you a product—to make them money. They want you to feel very comfortable with them. Always remember, they are salespeople. Be skeptical. It's no different than going to a car dealer. Even though you have a functioning car, the salesperson's intent is to sell you another. Or if you get your eyes examined at an optical chain, you will likely end up with new glasses. It's what they do! It's the same with many investment advisors. This doesn't mean they won't offer some good advice. But it does mean that you should research some alternatives and look closely at costs. Advisors are available who charge a flat fee or percentage of your assets and who don't sell anything with a commission. Search for fee-only planners at napfa.org, the website of the National Association of Personal Financial Advisors. Advisors should be selected according to credentials, ethics, business practices, services, and fees.

When selecting an advisor, questions to ask include the following: Are you a fee-based advisor? How are fees determined? Other than fees, what other charges will I incur? Are you compensated by any other sources? Are you compensated when you recommend a particular investment product? Just as when you take a patient's history, sometimes you need to ask a question in many different ways to get a complete answer.

Ability to trust that your investment advisors have your best interest at heart is key. That requires transparency and understanding of fee structures. You will not know for certain whether that trust is warranted until time has passed and you scrutinize your investments.

Do not mix insurance and investing into one product. To quote the White Coat Investor,

> There are many insurance-related investment products such as cash-value life insurance [whole life] and annuities which allow you to transfer investing risks to the insurance company for some guarantees. Unfortunately, when you transfer risk, you also transfer the lion's share of the returns. These products tend to be complex and complexity favors the insurance company and its agents. The company doesn't invest in any magic investments you can't invest in yourself, but once the agent gets his commissions, the company pays its expenses and profits, and you pay for the costs of the insurance part of the policy, is there any surprise that the "investment" can't keep up with more traditional investments? [12]

If an investment advisor tries to sell me a whole life insurance policy or an annuity, it throws up a red flag, and I become very cautious about everything he or she suggests. It's my financial advisor litmus test.

It's possible to check broker compliance records at finra.org. Ask the advisor for his or her CRD (Central Registration Depository) number to make access to records easier.[13] FINRA is an independent, not-for-profit organization authorized by Congress to protect investors. In 2016, the entity brought 1,434 disciplinary actions against brokers and investment firms.

Most financial advisors have a series of letters after their name, such as ChFC, CLU, and CFP. These indicate certification and expertise in specific areas. Some designations are industry-based, and others result from passing a detailed examination. FINRA's website has a list of 174 of these acronyms. It can be quite confusing! Using this site, you can determine the issuing organization as well as any educational, certification, and continuing education requirements. A designation associated with the insurance industry, such as chartered life underwriter (CLU), gives a heads-up that the individual is an insurance salesperson. Following are the more prestigious, higher-rated credentials (whitecoatinvestor.com):

- CFP: certified financial planner
- CFA: chartered financial analyst
- ChFC: chartered financial consultant
- CPA/PFS: certified public accountant with additional personal financial specialist credentials.

Although I was given some advice by a local insurance/investment advisor that I did not consider appropriate, I am glad I did accept his recommendation to purchase a long-term care insurance policy. Though expensive, it reduces the financial risk of needing to pay for a large nursing bill.

Every few years I need to review investments with my financial advisors to ensure that there isn't a creep toward more expensive positions. Otherwise, my portfolio seemed to gradually become more expensive. If you are paying a large expense fee, have your advisors explain to you why they have placed you in that expensive alternative. Many large financial institutions have their own no-load mutual funds.

Even though they have fiduciary responsibility, you may be placed in one of their funds even if another highly rated fund with lower costs and a higher return is available. Is the difference between them significant enough to ask for a change?

14

Trading

I often had the urge to buy and sell stocks. This was usually stimulated by the media or friends discussing a fantastic opportunity: you can't miss! Buying a stock that is growing in value is a common temptation. Consider the value of a stock that has been rising tremendously over the past six months. We jump on the bandwagon only to find the value has reached its peak and then watch it decline in value for a while, always hoping for a resurgence in price. Eventually, we sell it for a loss. If you are going to purchase individual stocks, it is important to understand the fundamentals that are pushing up the stock of the company. Just buying it because it's going up in price and a friend recommends it is a recipe for disaster. In general, by the time we hear about a wildly successful stock, it is probably reaching its peak, and we are buying it from Wall Street types who are selling and taking the profit. The initial investors rely on us to push up the value so that they can sell. It is difficult to be a stock picker, expecting to make money. As physicians, we may feel we are smarter than others and can make this work, but we do not have the time or connections to understand the markets.

Every time stock is purchased or sold, there is a charge. Discount brokers are available online. They are generally cheaper than your stockbroker. According to NerdWallet.com, both TD Ameritrade and E*trade charge $9.99 a trade (as of 2017).[1] Merrill, a broker, charges only $6.95 a trade if the trade is done online, whereas it will cost $29.95 through a broker.[2] At Vanguard, the price varies with how much is invested with Vanguard. With less than $50,000, the first twenty-five online trades are $7.00 each. A portfolio of $1,000,000 gets you twenty-five free trades.[3] If you are a trader, do it at a low cost. Charges can add up!

Trading can be expensive. It is certainly highly unpredictable. The buying and selling fees alone will remove some of your profit. Buying small amounts of stock is particularly dangerous. Let's imagine that you purchase $100 of stock in corporation X via TD Ameritrade. At a later date, you decide to sell. You just incurred two $9.99 fees for that opportunity. The stock would have had to rise in value 20 percent for you to break even, and taxes are due on the income generated. Obviously, with larger purchases this is not as significant a problem, but it still will take significant growth in the value of a stock to make it worthwhile.

Imagine that in February 2008 you had $100,000 in the stock market. Subsequently, the value of the market dropped 43 percent. The new worth of your portfolio, $57,000, made you panic, and you removed your assets from the market. How would you know when to return to the market? Most likely, you would regain confidence after a substantial market rise. Although you lost 43 percent, to return to the amount you had prior to the collapse, you would need the market now to rise 86 percent. Removing the assets and not returning them to the market until much of the recovery has occurred makes it very difficult to make up the needed 86 percent gain. It is almost impossible to time the market. The usual result is buying high and selling low—not a recommended way to grow your resources. Sure, there are people who occasionally time it perfectly, and they make certain you know about it, like the time I removed my children's college funds from the market just before the 2000 crash. People rarely tell you when they have lost money, but they are quick to tell you when they clean up. Even professional Wall Street investors can't time the market on a regular basis. Don't think you can. Try to be a long-term investor, a passive investor who doesn't interfere in the day-to-day of investing.

The Dalbar Quantitative Analysis of Investor Behavior Report (QAIB) has examined investor returns for the past thirty years.[4] The conclusion of its 2017 report is that "investment results are more dependent on investor behavior than on fund performance. Mutual fund investors who hold on to their investments are more successful than those who time the market." The average diversified stock fund grew 8.3 percent in 2014. The Dalbar Report determined that the average investor return was only 5.5 percent as a result of not staying in the market. Even more dramatic losses were found with bond investors. Fear prompts sale of investments when value is declining, and greed motivates their purchase during periods of growth. Again, buying high and selling low is not a successful strategy. Avoid trying to time the market. It cannot be done.

The best way to invest is to contribute regularly so that you will catch all the buying opportunities. Of the twenty-six million Americans who had a 401(k) plan at the end of 2007, only four million continued to contribute to their plans consistently until 2013. This group saw their investments grow four times larger than those who left the market.[5]

Perhaps you are too afraid to put your savings in the market and instead keep it all in the bank, in a guaranteed deposit. Ric Edelman, in his book *Rescue Your Money*, shows that on December 31, 2015, $100,000 invested in a bank certificate of deposit paying 0.8 percent annually returned $800 a year in interest. Assuming a 30 percent tax bracket, the real interest rate growth was 0.56 percent.[6] Extrapolated over the next twenty years and assuming a 2.3 percent inflation rate, the investment would lose 1.74 percent a year, resulting in a balance of $65,200. Still want to keep your assets in the bank?

We all have observed the daily rising and falling of the stock market.

It was particularly nerve-racking to see it drop to the extent it did in 2008. It is understandable to want to avoid the bad times and jump on board for the good times. But no one can identify these times with any accuracy. You must stay invested to catch the growth spells. Over time, the market has always gone up a little more than it goes down. When prices start to decline, get excited! It's a buying opportunity. Your regular purchases will catch the lower prices and produce growth in your portfolio.

Why invest in mutual funds and ETFs? Because they are safer! "For the five years preceding December 31, 2015 only 49 percent of stocks on the New York Stock Exchange made money," whereas 99 percent of mutual funds did[7]. They are diversified and contain hundreds to thousands of securities, which allows gains and losses to average out better than individual stocks.

If you really want to play the market by trading in individual stocks, consider creating a small investment account with a low-cost broker. Place a few thousand dollars in this account to "play" with. Keep it totally separate from other investments, and never place retirement assets or other important financial reserves in it. Buy and sell all you want as long as you stay within the limited funding of the account. It's likely that after a while you will become bored. I did. My account is currently inactive, awaiting the reawakening of my interest.

Twenty years ago, Amazon stock was worth about $2.00 a share on a split adjusted basis. Today, its basis is around $997. This is a 36 percent compounded annual gain. Ten thousand dollars invested then would be worth about $5 million today. During this time period Amazon stock has had 199 daily declines of 6 percent or more and 107 different occasions where the stock declined by 15 percent. In December 1999, Amazon shares lost 95 percent of their value during the dot-com bubble.[8] If you watched your stocks closely, would you have stayed invested in Amazon during any of these downturns? How nervous would you have been during those declines? Sometimes it doesn't pay to watch the market too closely.

The market can vary a percentage point or so on a daily basis. Once you have a million dollars in your account, $10,000 can easily disappear on a given day. It usually reappears a short time later when the market goes back up, but it can be scary. If you are fainthearted, perhaps it's not a good idea to look at the market indices or your investments every day—probably not even every week. It could make you nervous and itchy to sell!

15

Protect Yourself against the Unknown

Any number of unforeseen expenses can occur in our lives. For the small, simple ones such as an air conditioner breaking down, we basically self-insure and pay the expense ourselves. Having a three- to six-month emergency fund is helpful to pay for those occurrences. Some risks are not insurable, such as a sexual harassment suit or loss of your job. Most major exposures can be protected by insurance, and five major types are essential to preserving income and assets:

1. Life insurance. There are two major reasons to have life insurance. The primary reason is to protect your family in the case of an untimely death. Insurance creates an income to support your spouse and children so that they won't need to do something drastic such as sell the home or place the children in childcare while the surviving spouse returns to work. In most cases this need lasts only twenty to thirty years. Once the children have left home and the mortgage has been paid, expenses dramatically drop. A life insurance policy may no longer be needed. At some point in time, you also will have

accumulated enough financial resources to basically self-insure. I have ten more years remaining on a term life insurance policy. That additional money, should I die, probably won't change my wife's lifestyle. We have saved enough for a comfortable life. But until you get to that point, life insurance is essential.

Most fee-based planners recommend a guaranteed term insurance policy. This policy is strictly insurance. There is no investment portion attached. It's generally very inexpensive and certainly cheaper if you are healthy. Lock in the premiums for twenty to thirty years. Purchase it through a highly rated company. The least expensive may not be the best. You don't want to be in a position where the company goes out of business and you have to buy a new policy later at higher premiums. If someone tries to sell you an insurance-based investment product such as whole life, universal life, or cash-value insurance, be very cautious. When a financial advisor suggests a whole life or similar product, that indicates to me that my other investments may also have high costs associated with them. Scrutiny is advised. Perhaps it is time to look for a new advisor. These plans are very expensive, and the return on your investment is unlikely to be better than what you can get from the market. A $1,000,000 term policy for a healthy thirty-five-year-old white male is $1,160 annually, whereas a whole life policy for the same amount is $13,440 a year.[1] Much of that large whole life premium goes to the salesman as a commission.

The second reason to have life insurance is to assist in paying death taxes or a major financial obligation that continues after death. For instance, your business partner may have a life insurance policy on you so that if you die, he or she can purchase your portion of the business easily. This is often stipulated in the partnership agreement.

The recent increase in the federal estate tax exemption to $5,450,000 per person allows a couple with assets of twice that amount to be excluded from federal "death" taxes. As a result, only 0.2 percent of individuals pay these taxes, reducing the need for life insurance.[2]

2. Disability insurance. This insurance protects income from a disability that prevents employment. It is essential part of your financial armor.

3. Home and auto insurance. These policies protect you from liability and excessive health costs in relation to events involving your automobile and home.

4. Umbrella policy. An umbrella policy is liability insurance that extends beyond the limits of your home and automobile coverage. It adds an additional layer of security and may cover situations your other policies don't. It is commonly purchased by individuals with a high net worth and an increased risk of being sued.

5. Long-term care insurance. This insurance is vital, as we age, to assist in management of costs associated with nursing care. It is an excellent mechanism to help conserve assets in retirement. With increasing life spans, it is almost certain that you or your spouse will require extended nursing care. The median cost of a nursing home is $92,000 a year.[3] A friend recently told me it is costing $10,500 a month as of 2017 ($126,000/year) for her mother to be cared for in a local extended-care facility. This can obviously decimate retirement assets. A long-term care policy can be a lifesaver for a surviving spouse, not only financially but also mentally and emotionally.

Policies are not cheap. They increase in cost yearly. The earlier purchased, the better. Most policies today cover only three to four years. Inflation riders are suggested.

One last thing! Just as you perform yearly continuing medical education, you should also participate in continuing financial education. Let's call it CFE. As you start the process of building your retirement plan, read about personal finance. Perhaps go to a few seminars. (Watch out for the salespeople.) Ask questions of friends and mentors. Peruse personal finance journals and websites. Read financial blogs such as the White Coat Investor. Think of it as studying for your boards. Afterward, continue the process yearly. Keep up-to-date.

16

Financial Summary

The entire purpose of this book has been to highlight the need for retirement saving and to suggest some ways to safely achieve that goal. In most cases you will not have the opportunities previous generations have had to secure themselves financially by utilizing generous retirement plans and selling practice assets. Achieving financial success will require planning and perseverance. The following steps are critical to achieving success.

1. Determine your financial needs for retirement. Create a plan.
2. Save money.
   a. Maximize contributions in tax-deferred plans.
   b. Maximize employer contributions.
   c. Use Roth investments if income allows.
   d. Save money outside of formal retirement plans.

3. Ask your advisor about the costs associated with all investments.
4. Use low-cost investments.
5. Be disciplined.
   a. Start immediately.

b. Invest regularly in the appropriate amount.

c. Control living expenses.

d. Be a long-term, passive investor. Don't try to time the market.

6. Use fiduciary and fee-based planners. Avoid salespeople.

7. Insure against adversity:

a. Life insurance. In most cases twenty- to thirty-year term life is adequate.

b. Disability insurance.

c. Home and auto with high liability limits.

d. Umbrella policy.

e. Long-term care insurance.

8. Continue your financial education.

This may seem complex and difficult. It really isn't. Your advisors will assist you. Once your system is up and running, it will be on autopilot.

The most important part of the entire program is to get started as soon as possible! You are almost a decade behind your peers! To quote Ben Franklin, "Time is money."

17

Physicians Don't Save Money

During a recent conversation with my trust advisor at a large national bank, I asked why the bank doesn't approach young physicians before the physicians have acquired the requisite millions needed to invest with the bank. That way the bank could get them started in its system early, before competitors such as insurance people and brokers latch onto them. Certainly, these high-wage earners would make great candidates as clients. I was surprised when he suggested to me that it was not worth the effort. "Physicians," he said, "tend to be poor clients."

"Why?" I asked incredulously. "They have large salaries and certainly need ethical and expert help in managing their investments."

"Yes," he agreed, "they certainly have great incomes, but they don't tend to save much." He emphasized, "Doctors don't have money. They spend it all." He went on to say that of his many clients, only a handful were physicians. The majority of his millionaires were small business people. He hypothesized that perhaps those individuals appreciate the capriciousness of business and save for a less predictable future. Their understanding of the importance of investing and planning in their business follows through to their personal life.

This lack of spending control has resulted in physicians in their late fifties and early sixties being unprepared financially for retirement. Some haven't accumulated even a million dollars—clearly an insufficient amount to retire in the style of life to which they are accustomed. Many physicians at that age are scurrying to accumulate the additional resources needed to retire. At an age where they should be slowing down, they are working as hard as or harder than ever. Should a personal medical or professional complication occur, their finances would be devastated. I wish a better future for you.

How and why does this occur? There is no simple answer as to why physicians don't save at a similar rate to their peers in other industries. Perhaps in some cases it results from feelings of deprivation during the years of delayed gratification while the person went through medical school and residency. Some never learn good financial habits. During the sudden jump in income from resident to attending, many lose the financial balance they had while in training and get seduced by, shall I say, the "dark side."

Physicians' wages are fairly safe from the ups and downs of the economy. From year to year, doctors continue to have fairly stable incomes. If they spend more than intended, additional resources will be coming next month—and the next month and the next month—to resolve the debt. With the exception of a few specialties, doctors don't need to reinvest large sums of money in their businesses for equipment and growth. But when they do not get in the habit of saving money or investing in their business, that money is instead spent on lifestyle and "stuff." Subconsciously, they think more income will come next year, so why worry? This flawed thought process results in unfulfilled financial goals.

It's not uncommon for physicians to invest in something they don't have the knowledge or time to manage. They continue to throw money at the investment as it struggles rather than investing the time or expertise needed to correct the management issues. This is a guaranteed way to lose money. Watch out for your ego telling you that you are smarter than everyone else and can make something a success when others have not.

Physicians are often given special attention by financial institutions. The average physician has an easier time qualifying for loans than the general public. By the time they have graduated from medical school, they have already received hundreds of thousands of dollars in student loans without the loaner demanding collateral, a cosigner, or a business plan. No similar program exists for someone starting a business.

When a physician enters practice, many financial institutions have special "new doctor" mortgage programs with special rates, smaller down payments, and no PMI (private mortgage insurance) requirement. They sometimes remove the jumbo home penalty. Some allow a loan repayment–to–income rate of up to 50 percent and don't include student loan debt in that calculation.[1] It's absurd, like giving narcotics to a junky. These plans encourage physicians to purchase expensive homes. With a larger home come higher property taxes, more furniture, and larger utility bills. Home insurance is greater. It is likely the home will be in a more exclusive neighborhood where "keeping up with the Joneses" is a prevalent mindset. Premium cars, private schools, and a vacation home become a must. These great "deals" seduce us to borrow more money. The financial industry's goal is profit. It readily manipulates physicians to achieve this goal. Being aware of this manipulation is the first step to financial freedom.

It is wonderful to receive lower-cost mortgages! Certainly, take advantage of them. They become a problem only when physicians are encouraged by these low costs to purchase a home that is too large and doesn't fit into long-term financial goals. A home, with all its associated expenses, is always going to cost more than you think.

I recently became aware of a financial advisor who recommended that a new family doctor purchase a $600,000 home rather than one costing $400,000. He explained that the family would save money because they would receive a larger mortgage interest deduction on their income taxes. That they would have a larger tax deduction is certainly true, but to spend hundreds of thousands of dollars more to get only several extra thousand dollars of interest deduction would be crazy. The added payments, property tax, utilities, and additional furniture required would easily eclipse the tax deduction.

I ran some numbers. The first-year interest payments on a $400,000 fifteen-year mortgage at 3.65 percent would total $14,165. For a $600,000 mortgage, the first-year interest would be $21,243: a $7,078 variation. Monthly payments on the first home would be $2,884, and on the second, $4,326: a $1,442-per-month difference.

According to the mortgage tax deduction calculator at bankrate. com, a married couple filing jointly in the 25 percent tax bracket would receive tax savings of $5,113 on a $400,000 home and $7,670 on a $600,000 home. The difference between the two is $2,557. Purchasing the larger home, you would pay $17,304 more in payments a year to get $2,557 in savings on your taxes. Does that sound like a good deal?

Property taxes for a $400,000 home in my community are $8,503. For a $600,000 home they are $12,754. Wow! The difference between the two homes' property taxes is $4,251. Just the additional property tax cancels out the benefit from the income tax mortgage deduction. I haven't added the many other expenses that will also increase with a more expensive home. Can a comfortable life be experienced in a $400,000 home? Certainly, in the Midwest and probably in most areas of the country. Some areas of the coasts are an exception.

This discussion brings to the forefront two premier concepts of living and business: (1) Keep your overhead as low as possible. (2) Do the math—on all investments. Don't believe other people, particularly salespeople. You want to know how the expense will affect you personally.

A thousand dollars a month just to pay for the taxes on a home worries me. No, it scares me. I am retired with a fixed income I don't want that much overhead!

Assuming a $200,000 annual salary and the purchase of a $400,000 home, how much money will you have to live on after some basic expenses? After you defer $54,000 a year for retirement, taxable income is $146,000. Subtract approximately $30,000 a year for student loan payments, and you now have $116,000. A year of mortgage payments amounting to $35,000 costs about $29,495 after tax savings. US income tax and SS and Medicare tax come to about $50,000 ($49,270). Subtract Michigan state income tax of 4.2 percent ($6,132), and the remaining take-home income is approximately $31,103.

When you realize you have to live on $31,103 a year for everything else, you can now start to determine the true effect spending has on your lifestyle and how much you want to allocate to each expenditure. Please don't go into debt. Watch out for excessive credit card spending. You have about six hundred dollars a week to spend. That is actually quite a bit of money.

That dinner out with drinks with your spouse once a week costing $60, 10 percent of your remaining income, is definitely worth the expenditure. But can the same be said for the $1,500 spent annually on a daily latte at Starbucks?

It's difficult to set long-term spending goals unless you know where your money goes. You can carefully keep track with paper and pencil or, more likely, an app or computer program. Many exist. It may be beneficial to discuss this with your financial advisor and ask savvy friends what they are using.

There is a culture among physicians in which lifestyle is emphasized. Partially explained by the guile of the financial industry to encourage consumption, it is exacerbated by the fact that most physicians tend to associate closely with other high-income physicians. There is little opportunity for outside influences to bring financial reason to their world. The mindset is to think in the present. Money comes easily. "Keeping up with the Joneses" can become the norm, and it's hard to discern when life priorities are a little distorted. If moderation isn't achieved, substantial shortages will occur in retirement plans, and physicians will be working longer into what should be the quiet, relaxing years of retirement. We live in a protected cocoon. It's time to break out. The biggest barrier to becoming rich is living like you're rich before you are.

It is clear that many pressures are placed upon physicians to spend money, whether by friends, financial advisors, or financial institutions. This is a force that you need to be aware is washing over you every day. Otherwise, you become similar to a drug addict looking for the next fix instead of thinking about the future thirty years from now. Wealth creation is a result not of how much you earn but rather how much you save.

18

Practice, Practice, Practice

Earlier I discussed the concept that physician reimbursement is likely to be flat in the coming decades. Medicare has already indicated that it doesn't plan to pay physicians significantly more in the next ten years, and it is changing its reimbursement plan to an indecipherable hodgepodge of regulations and bonuses. Physicians are an expense, and significant pressures exist to control all health care expenses (except, it seems, health care administrators). It's possible that reimbursement for services will decline. Best-case scenario, it stays flat. But even if reimbursement remains flat, real income will lose value as a result of inflation.

With these assumptions, it is important that you, as a physician, be as skilled as possible upon completing your residency. Why? Three reasons. First, it's the right thing to do, to give the best care possible. Second, you thus can maximize your income early on in your career while reimbursement is high and inflation hasn't occurred. Finally, the increased skills and confidence will stay with you the rest of your life, heightening the types, volume, and quality of surgery and patient care you perform throughout your life (which also affects your income).

The better your skills, the higher your income. Though we didn't necessarily go into medicine to earn the highest wages, high income will help pay off your loans and allow you to save for retirement. Too much money? There are plenty of charities that can use your help.

I have seen numerous physicians take years to acquire the necessary skills to become successful physicians after residency. Several have given up practicing in their chosen surgical field due to lack of confidence and poor surgical skills. I don't want this to be you. It will limit your income and your ability to purchase a practice or be offered a partnership. Better to be competent right out of the box. Contrary to your residency in-service exam, it's not just medical knowledge that makes you a great physician. Please don't misunderstand me: medical knowledge is crucial. But it is only a portion of the total package required to be a successful.

If you are training to be a surgeon, you will have spent at least the past twenty-five years of your life in school and residency, getting to the point where you can operate competently. What a waste if, upon graduation, you cannot perform the standard procedures of your field confidently and successfully. It is crucial to make every effort to be the best you can be upon finishing your residency. This seems obvious, and to most it is, but every year I hear of someone struggling with his or her skills in practice.

It's unlikely you will be a phenomenal surgeon at graduation. It will take years for you to feel truly confident. Thirty years into practice, you will still be improving and perfecting your skills. The only way to become confident and competent is to participate in every procedure you can while a resident. There will be times when you think, *I've done a hundred of these. I don't need to do another.* Yes, you do. Every patient is different. You want to see every possible complication. We have all heard the adage about needing ten thousand hours of experience to be highly skilled at something. How can you be great if you don't get your ten thousand hours in? Two weeks ago, after having performed thousands of routine retrobulbar blocks, I had my first retrobulbar hemorrhage. It's a potentially blinding situation requiring immediate attention. The resident on my service had the opportunity to perform a lateral canthotomy and manage the situation. It's something you only read about. If he had said, "I've seen a thousand blocks; I don't need to see another," he never would have had the opportunity to witness this rare condition and surgically treat it.

Most surgical programs now have a simulator available. All have the ability to get tissue, either human or animal, upon which to practice. These kinds of practice count toward your ten thousand hours of skill development only if you are using proper technique. Rick Pitino, national champion basketball coach at Louisville, emphasizes the necessity of practicing at all times with the proper form.[1] It is of no value to shoot a thousand free throws improperly. In fact, it's a detriment. You need to do things correctly so they are second nature. Remember the first time you drove a car? The amount of concentration it took? The exhaustion you felt? Now after thousands of hours of driving, it comes so naturally that you are hardly aware of what you are doing. That's the goal.

It is frustrating when a resident is allowed the opportunity to perform a surgery and then struggles. It's annoying to later find out the resident had not practiced on the simulator or animal tissue. Am I likely to give that resident much opportunity in the future? The more a resident can do competently, the more he or she will be allowed to do. The way to start this cascade is to practice. When I was a medical student struggling to sew up a bloody episiotomy, my attending was yelling at me, "How do you get to Carnegie Hall, how do you get to Carnegie Hall?" I looked up at him, befuddled. "Practice, practice, practice," he said.

Recently, one of my residents struggled during several cases. I knew she was trying hard, but things were not clicking. That afternoon, without my suggestion, she drove an hour to access a surgical simulator and spent four hours improving her skills. The next time I worked with her, she was noticeably improved. Another struggling resident was having trouble with anxiety and tremors during surgery. She analytically evaluated the situation and determined that a beta-blocker was required to stifle those problems, and she has since become an excellent, confident surgeon. When I see these kinds of efforts, I am much more likely to go out of my way to assist that resident.

Psychosocial skills are critical in dealing with patients. It's important that you be as empathetic as possible while trying to get a concise history, do a physical exam, review the chart, and instruct the patient in disease management, all the while typing in the electronic medical record (EMR). Did I mention that you need to do this in ten to fifteen minutes? Residency is the time to sharpen these skills so that upon completion you can hit the ground running. Being able to see a full patient load immediately upon starting employment will improve your chances of receiving a bonus!

It takes time for skills to develop. Some are faster than others. It's expected that you will be slow and methodical as a first-year resident, but by the time you are a senior resident, your skills should be honed. When looking at residencies, consider one in which you will have a gradual increase in patient volume in the clinic over the years, ending up with the volume a physician would see in private practice. This will prepare you for the real world.

It's all about conscious practice—every day, every visit, every surgery. How can I get better? Observe successful physicians. What are their secrets? What makes their bedside manner so appealing? What techniques do they use to get to the substance of the interview? How do they exit from an exam? Try to get out of the clinic and visit successful doctors in the community.

Develop pet phrases and discussions regarding the major diseases you come in contact with so that you can rattle them off even while doing something else (such as typing into the EMR). Standardized phrases are great. You repeat them to everyone. If a patient says, "You never told me that," you can be assured you did.

Completing your residency ready for the real world will pay countless dividends. In this time of flat to declining reimbursement, you will be able to efficiently see a full day of patients and be ready for more. Surgical skills will deliver a high level of success with fewer complications. Your income will be stable and likely will grow, allowing you to fully fund a retirement plan and pay off your school loans. Stress levels will be reduced. Patients will learn to trust you. Employers won't need to pressure you to produce. Life will be good!

Once you finish your training, you are not done improving. You are not the best physician you can possibly be. You will never be perfect. Every day, you should strive to be a better doctor and improve your skills. Your education should never stop. As you get further and further away from training, your skills naturally atrophy, interest wanes, and life interferes. Extraordinary efforts, discipline, and organization will be required to slow that atrophy.

19

Protect Yourself

Having adequate insurance and retirement savings is critically important to asset and lifestyle protection. Understanding how to invest by maximizing returns and reducing risk is important for a successful retirement plan. We have many types of insurance to control for unknown perils.

Disability insurance protects your income should you become disabled. It is very important. But there is often a ninety-day waiting period before you receive support, and the benefits are generally less than your wages. Consequently, you really don't want to become disabled if you can help it. Ninety days of lost income can create significant financial strain.

Our vocation requires a high level of mental ability, physical conditioning, excellent vision, and fine motor skills. Loss of any of these could markedly affect our ability to practice and support our families. Preventing disabilities, injuries, and illness for ourselves should become a major goal. As physicians, you are well aware of the benefits of exercise, diet, moderation in lifestyle and the need to avoid smoking. In a way, maximizing appropriate healthy behaviors is a kind of insurance policy that can help physicians maintain an active career.

Once we are aware of the risks associated with our activities, many injuries and health problems are preventable. My grandfather lost three fingers on his right hand from a circular saw accident. As a surgeon, I depend on my hands. Without them I would need to find a new career, and my income would be severely reduced. Consequently, I have consciously avoided dangerous pieces of equipment, such as circular saws, in an attempt to extend my career. As a resident, I broke several fingers playing volleyball and was unable to operate for a month. Imagine the loss of income had I been in practice. Not surprisingly, I no longer play volleyball. Having injured my hands on multiple occasions while gardening, I now wear gloves. As an ophthalmologist, I am constantly reminded to wear protective eyewear. I wear a helmet and bright colors when cycling. What precautions should you take to preserve and extend your career?

In her book *Grit: The Power of Passion and Perseverance*, Angela Duckworth quotes the extreme measures that Hall of Fame pitcher Tom Seaver described going to in order to maintain his level of excellence: "Pitching … determines what I eat, when I go to bed, what I do while I'm awake. It determines how I spend my life when I'm not pitching … If it means I have to remind myself to pet dogs with my left hand or throw logs in the fire with my left hand, then I do that, too. If it means in the winter I eat cottage cheese instead of chocolate chip cookies in order to keep my weight down, then I eat cottage cheese."

We have all spent decades and hundreds of thousands of dollars to become physicians. We can lose our career in a blink of an eye. Protect your investment. It's the cheapest insurance plan you can buy! Are there any activities you should avoid? Any precautions you should take? What protective devices should you be using? Do you wear safety glasses? A little effort and planning will extend and possibly save your career.

20

Personal Habits

We have determined that to be able to accumulate sufficient assets for a successful retirement, you will need to save about $54,000 a year for the next thirty-five years. As you age, it's essential that you continue to be productive at a very high level for many years to achieve this goal. Doing this will require excellent physical and mental health. As a physician, you are well aware of the many benefits that exercise and a proper diet provide to your quality of life. Sleep is essential. It can be difficult to discipline yourself to maintain standards in these areas when you are extremely busy practicing medicine and raising a family. But if you can dedicate even a small amount of time to exercise, mindfulness, and diet, your chances of retiring successfully will be much greater. If you don't take care of yourself, how will you care for others?

World Health Organization and Centers for Disease Control guidelines recommend 150 minutes of moderate to intensive aerobic physical activity a week along with two episodes of strength training.[1] This exercise can take many forms. It is important for you to find a program that fits you and your lifestyle so that you can make it a regular habit. Habit is key! You may not feel that you need some conditioning at age thirty, but I can guarantee it will improve your life, and once you reach your fifties, you will be glad you took the time. Starting early has so many benefits!

Our days are busy. We rush from exam room to exam room, hospital to office. At the end of the day, we are physically and mentally exhausted. We ask ourselves, "How can I keep doing this for the next three decades?" After a busy day, I would come home barely able to walk. I couldn't hold a conversation. If I sat down, I would fall asleep immediately.

Once we purchased a cross-country ski machine, my life changed. With the machine placed in our bedroom, I tried to use it every night for a minimum of twenty minutes. It was as if someone had flipped a switch. My energy returned. I became a member of the family again. It didn't take much time—no need to drive to a club and put on workout clothes adequate for public viewing. I also didn't have to go out in the cold during the winter or the heat and humidity in the summer. My children and wife would often visit me while I was working out, and when they didn't, I could watch TV or read a book. Over the years my time on the ski machine increased to forty minutes a day (about the time it takes to watch a period of hockey). I found I could see fifty to sixty patients in the office and no longer be tired. Stress associated with surgery was markedly reduced.

As physicians, we depend on our mental abilities. We worry that as we age, we will lose some of these cognitive skills. Exercise has been shown to help maintain memory, improve learning, and delay the onset of Alzheimer's. It reduces the incidence of depression and improves alertness.

In addition to perhaps extending life span by five years, the list of benefits from exercise is long. Additional bonuses include the following:[2]

- Maintenance of strength
- Stronger bones and increased bone density
- Reduction of injuries and falls
- Improved balance and mobility

- Improved appearance
- Faster metabolism
- Improved cardiovascular health and reduced LDL
- Improved energy
- Help with controlling weight
- Slowing of the deterioration of muscle that comes with aging
- Boosts to the immune system
- Improved blood pressure
- Better sleep patterns
- Less diabetes
- Reduced risk of some cancers
- Improved symptoms of menopause
- Relief of arthritis and back pain
- Reduced incidence of stroke

The need to eat a healthy diet goes hand in hand with exercise. You are all aware of what that means. I will not go into much discussion other than to encourage you to control your calories, avoid fads, eat fruits and vegetables and lean meat, and avoid trans fats. Don't forget to drink plenty of fluids, but try to avoid those that are calorie-laden. There is mounting evidence that "diet" soda actually stimulates you to be hungrier. As with everything, buyer beware.

Times have changed. Physicians used to be included in discussions regarding practice and hospital management issues. Reimbursement equations change yearly. Paper charts were simple and inexpensive, but now complicated and expensive EMRs are mandated. We cannot change edicts from high! Try not to focus on things you cannot control. They will drive you crazy! Shift your concentration to issues in which you can make a difference.

The financial benefits of being healthy are so numerous that it would take a book to discuss them all. But you will certainly be able to see more patients, miss fewer days of work, and have reduced medical bills and smaller insurance payments.

What good will a pile of money do you if you are unable to use it because you ignored your health? Retirement will be much more enjoyable if you can be physically active, run around with your grandchildren, and travel. The way to get there is to exercise, eat right, and practice mindfulness. Just as in saving for your retirement, you need to start these habits early and continue on a regular schedule throughout your life. Discipline is required.

21

Summary

You have adapted to the current changes in medical practice. New permutations of health care will evolve, and you will adapt to those also. It's uncertain what the practice of medicine will look like in the future. One thing is certain: your financial prospects will not be as generous as you expect.

Most of you will be employed physicians working for large hospital systems or enormous medical groups. As a result, there will be less ability to adjust your practice to accommodate for decreased or flat reimbursement. Productivity and innovation will be restricted. The formal retirement plans available to you will not allow you to invest enough to be able to retire comfortably. There will be no practice assets to sell. You will need to save for retirement on your own. This will require willpower, planning, and lifestyle adjustments. Your spouse will need to understand and be supportive.

Wages will be flat for most of your career. Those of you who can increase your productivity and see more patients will have some initial income growth. This is particularly true for procedure-oriented specialties. Within five to seven years, I expect that wage growth will slow and that you can expect less than a 1 percent expansion of your wages yearly until you retire. By that time your inflation-adjusted wages could be half to two-thirds of what they are today. Don't be surprised if your nurses and medical assistants get larger yearly wage increases than you do. At the end of your residency, allow for some lifestyle "creep," but avoid an explosion. While you still have the income, make every effort to pay off debts as soon as possible. Except for a reasonable mortgage, avoid initiating new long-term debt. Try not to buy something with the expectation that your wages will grow to cover the payments.

You could easily live another thirty years after you retire. Maintaining a modest income stream during that time will require substantial retirement savings, probably about eight million dollars. A 4 percent yearly withdrawal from this account should allow for a comfortable, consistent income for three decades. Achieving this retirement goal will require investing at least $54,000 a year for thirty-five years at a 7 percent growth rate—a huge sum! Social Security contributions are uncertain. Try not to be reliant on them.

If you cannot save this amount, you will need to either work longer or reduce your standard of living. Working longer requires optimization of physical and mental health. Excellent exercise, diet, and sleep habits are a must. Obviously, you should avoid excessive alcohol and drugs. Don't smoke.

Keep the costs of your investments low by utilizing a low-cost financial advisor, preferably one with fiduciary responsibility. Don't try to time the market. Diversify your investments. Beware of financial advisors who want to sell you an annuity or whole life insurance. Try not to prematurely access your retirement savings for toys or the expenses of daily living.

I am certain that with planning and sacrifice you will be able to finance a successful retirement.

Finally, as *Kiplinger's* outlines, it is easy to go broke in retirement if you do the following:[1]

1. Avoid stocks in investments because you are concerned with too much risk. The result: not enough growth.
2. Place all your investments in stocks because you want aggressive growth. Downturns in the market can devastate your portfolio.
3. Have a large percentage of your assets in one investment or stock. Remember Enron employees?
4. Live too long.
5. Spend too much.
6. Rely on Social Security alone. It is the primary source of retirement income in 61 percent of retirees but is not enough to support you in retirement. By 2035 it is projected to pay only 77 percent of promised benefits.
7. Be unable to work until retirement age. Sixty percent of workers leave the workforce earlier than planned. This can result in your not accumulating the resources needed and spending those you have prior to retirement age.
8. Get sick and spend your resources on health and nursing care.
9. Have your financial advisor place you in high-cost investments, reducing potential return.
10. Handle your investment accounts poorly. Pay penalties for not taking distribution at the proper time. Take Social Security too early. Remove money first from pretax savings.
11. Forget you owe taxes.
12. Bankroll your kids, giving your children the money you need to survive.
13. Be underinsured, on health, auto, home, liability, long-term care, and umbrella.
14. Get scammed. The National Counsel for Elder Abuse says that 55 percent of time, such abuse is performed by family or caregivers.

Notes

Chapter 1

1   Kupfer, Joel, "The Graying of US Physicians: Implications for Quality and Future Supply of Physicians," JAMA. 2016; 314(4): 341 doi: 10.1001/ Jama.2015,18248

2   "16ᵗʰ Annual Transamerica Retirement Survey: A Compendium of Findings about American Workers", accessed May 2017, https://www. TransamericaCenter.org/retirement-research/16ᵗʰ-Annual-retirement-survey/ retirement-survey-compendium.

3   " Twelve Reasons you will go broke in Retirement", accessed April 2017, https:// www.Kiplinger.com/Slideshow/retirement/T047-S001-12-reasons-you-will-go-broke-in-retirement/index.html

4   "2106 Meritt Hawkins Survey of American Physicians: Physician Practice Patterns and Perspectives", accessed April 2016, https://www.merritthawkins. com/physicians-foundation-survey.aspx

5   "Percentage of Current Income Needed in Retirement", 9/25/11, whitecoatinvestor.com/percentage-of-income-needed-in-retirement/

6   Andrew Dugan, "Retirement Remains Americas' Top Financial Worry", April 22, 2014, https://news.gallop.com/poll/1686/retirement-remains-americans-top-financial-worry.aspx

7   "2016 AMA Insurance Report on US Physicians Financial Preparedness", accessed May 2016, https://www.amainsure.com?reports/2016-financial-preparedness-practicing-physicians/index.html?page=14

8   "The Future ain't what it used to be", accessed October 2017, https:// wwwgoodreads.com/quotes24700-the-future-ain-t-what-it-used-to-be

9   globalrichlist.com, last accessed October 2017.

Chapter 2

1   "Time-Tested Tactics to Build Your Wealth", last accessed April 2017, https:// www.Kiplinger.com/slideshow/investing/T023-S002-time-tested-tactics-to-build-your-wealth/index.html

2   Social Security Benefit Calculators, last accessed 10/2017, https://www.ssa.gov/ oact/quickcalc/

3   "Employee Benefit Research Institute-2016 Retirement Confidence Survey-2016 Results", https://www.ebri.org/surveys/rcs/2016

4   Tim McMahon,"Long Term U.S. Inflation", April 1, 2014, https://inflationdata. com/inflation/inflation Rate/Long Term Inflation.asp

5   www.calculator.net/investment-calculator.html

Chapter 3

1   "2016 AMA Insurance Report on US Physicians Financial Preparedness", accessed May 2016, https://www.amainsure.com?reports/2016-financial-preparedness-practicing-physicians/index.html?page=14

Chapter 4

1   Ashley McGlone,"Merit-Based Incentive Payment System (MIPS), Https://www.ascrs.org/site/default/files/resourses/Merit-based Incentive Payment System(MIPS)_4_1_16.pdf

2   Peter J. McDonnell, "A wake-up call for physicians", Ophthalmology Times, vol. 42, no. 10, (June 15, 2017): 4

3   Academy Express, American Academy of Ophthalmology, March 2017, AAO.org

4   Https://www.cahabagba.com/part-b/enrollment-2/participating-vs-non-participating-part-b/

Chapter 5

1   https://www.irs.gov/newsroom/irs-announces-2017-pension-plan-limitations-401k-contributions-limit-remains-unchanged-at-18,000-for-2017

2   http://www-moneychimp.com/features/market_cagr.htm

3   The Economist, December 10, 2016, p.72

4   William Bengen, "Determining Withdrawal Rates using Historical Data", http://www.retailinvestor.org/pdf/Bengen1.pdf

5   https://www.irahelp.com/foram-post/12064-non-governmental-457b-money-what-are-my-concerns.

6   http://www.usinflationcalculator.com

7   http://www.irs.gov/retirement-plan/amount

Chapter 6

1   https://www.irs.gov/newsroom/irs-announces-2017-pension-plan-limitations-401k-contribution-limit-remains-unchanged-at-18000-for-2017

2   https://www.irs.gov/retirement-plans/retirement-plans-faqs-regarding-seps-contributions

Chapter 7

1 Vaclav Smil, "Two Decades Later: Nikkei and Lessons from the Fall," Dec 29,2009, http://www.aei.org/publication/two-decades-later-nikkei-and-lessons-from-the-fall/

2 https://www.marketwatch.com/investing/index/nik/historical?countrycode=jp,

Chapter 8

1 http://www.taxpolicycenter.org/sites/default/files/legacy/taxfacts/content/PDF/max_benefits.pdf

2 https://www.irs.gov/retirement-plans/choosing-a-retirement-plan-defined-benefit-plan

Chapter 9

1 http://www.bankrate.com/calculators/savings/moving-cost-of-living-calculator.aspx?s_kwcid=AL!1325!10!32176729000!300100275980&ef_id=WMROYwAABVknJWZ1:20171018144134:s

2 https://www.numbeo.com/cost-of-living/calculator.jsp

Chapter 10

1 Mitch Anthony, The New Retirementality (Wiley and Sons, 2014), 13.

2 https://obliviousinvestor.com/dividend-and-long-term-capital-gain-tax-rates/

Chapter 11

1 https://en.wikipedia.org/wiki/Health_savings_account

Chapter 12

1 http://www.snopes.com/quotes/einstein/interest.asp

2 http://www.moneychimp.com/features/market_cagr.htm

Chapter 13

1 https://www.thebalance.com/key-mutual-fund-terms-defined-2466595

2 https://en.wikipedia.org/wiki/Charles_D._Ellis

3 tps://about.vanguard.com/who-we-are/a-remarkable-history/ht

4   http://www.investopedia.com/terms/e/etf.asp

5   Ric Edelman, Rescue Your Money,(Simon and Schuster, 2016), 169

6   https://investor.vanguard.com/mutual-funds/low-cost

7   Ric Edelman, Rescue Your Money, (Simon and Schuster, 2016), 160

8   https://legal-dictionary.thefreedictionary.com/

9   https://www.looktowink.com/2017/09/dol-fiduciary-rule-explained-august-31-2017/

10 http://www.investmentnews.com/article/20160229/FREE/160229937/metlife-is-second-major-insurer-to-exit-the-brokerage-business-in

11 personal correspondence

12 https://www.whitecoatinvestor.com/the-10-commandments-of-the-white-coat-investor/8/13/12

13 http://www.finra.org/industry/registration-qualification

Chapter 14

1   https://www.nerdwallet.com/investing/best-online-broker/compare/etrade/td-ameritrade

2   https://www.nerdwallet.com/blog/investing/merrill-edge-review

3   https://investor.vanguard.com/financial-advisor/financial-advisor-fees

4   http://www.dalbar.com/QAIB/Index

5   Ric Edelman, Rescue Your Money, (Simon and Schuster, 2016), 37

6   Ric Edelman, Rescue Your Money, (Simon and Schuster, 2016), 16

7   Ric Edelman, Rescue Your Money, (Simon and Schuster, 2016), 164

8   https://www.wsj.com/news/author/7443

Chapter 15

1   https://life.statefarm.com/LifeQuote-web/customerquote/selectPolicy?conversationId=a5e827cf-b9ad-4fc7-83d0-fb3b86f110b3

2   https://www.cbpp.org/research/federal-tax/ten-facts-you-should-know-about-the-federal-estate-tax

3   http://www.kiplinger.com/article/retirement/T036-C032-S014-don-t-let-long-term-care-costs-ruin-retirement.html

Chapter 17

1   https://www.huntington.com/Personal/specialty-mortgages/physician-only-loan

Chapter 18

1   Rick Pitino, Overachieving in Business and Life, (Broadway Books,1998)

Chapter 20

1   https://ftgetsresults.wordpress.com/2010/12/28/world-health-organization-fitness-guidelines-for-adults/
2   http://time.com/4474874/exercise-fitness-workouts/

Chapter 21

1   http://www.kiplinger.com/

About the Author

Dr. Ralph P. Crew has been an ophthalmologist, emergency room physician, and general practitioner. He has been intimately involved with medical education for the past thirty years and is a clinical professor at Michigan State University. He retired from his practice in 2016 and dedicates his time to teaching residents and medical students. This is his first book.

Printed and bound by PG in the USA